Date Due

BRODART, INC.   Cat. No. 23 233   Printed in U.S.A.

English

The Preprofessional Major

Linwood E. Orange
University of Southern Mississippi

Fourth Edition, Revised

Library of Congress Cataloging-in-Publication Data
English, the preprofessional major.

Includes bibliographies.
1. Vocational guidance—United States. I. Title.
HF5382.5.U507 1986   378'.1942   85-31962
ISBN 0-87352-148-X

The Modern Language Association of America
10 Astor Place, New York 10003

ENGLISH: THE PREPROFESSIONAL MAJOR

Foreword

For several decades college education has drifted in the direction of increased specialization. Carefully planned and highly restricted curricula are prescribed for future engineers, business executives, physicians, lawyers, agronomists, and ecologists (to name only a few), and to an ever increasing extent the concept of a general liberal education is being crowded out of career preparation. After all, a liberal arts education is totally and hopelessly impractical, so why should students preparing for a professional career concern themselves with it?

Such thinking has inevitably led to the formulation of certain academic fallacies, one being that the English major is predestined to pedagogy and another, correspondingly, that the primary, perhaps sole, function of college English professors is to perpetuate their own species. The purpose of this booklet is to help put matters back into proper perspective by providing documentary evidence that training in English and literature, particularly at the college level, far from being a waste of time, is invaluable preparation for futures in four outstanding professional areas: law, medicine, business, and federal service.[1]

It is not, of course, the intention of this document to dissuade students majoring in English from choosing careers in education, which have provided a comfortable and satisfying livelihood for a great many dedicated people. Granted that the pay scale for teachers ranks low among the professions, compensation often takes other forms, such as the security of a steady income, a respectable status in the community, refuge from the fiercely competitive business world, advantageous group insurance and retirement fringe benefits, fellowship with those of kindred academic interests, ample vacation time (albeit some of it unpaid and unwanted), and, of course, the stimulating experience of contributing to the development of inquiring young minds. Further, the employment picture for new teachers, long a gloomy one, is now brightening with the advent of the progeny of the baby boom generation. Nevertheless, even in the best of times circumstances often prevent one from teaching, and those who are being or have been trained as educators would do well to keep informed about career alternatives. For them and for those of literary propensity who have never been tempted to indulge in pedagogy, this booklet is designed as a counseling guide.

The information on which the following discussion is based has been obtained by means of privately conducted surveys. Fifty-three law schools and thirty-seven medical schools (all fully accredited and highly reputable) located in twenty-one states, nearly four hundred industrial organizations of the "blue chip" variety, and forty-three governmental agencies contributed facts, figures, and comments.[2] Although a portion of the data was gathered as long ago as the fall of 1969, the validity of the earliest responses has been continually verified by ongoing communication with the areas concerned and by such studies as that of S. S. Stollman of the University of Windsor English department, who conducted surveys of law schools, medical schools, and businesses in Canada, with results closely corresponding to those set forth here.

For purposes of this survey, it was made clear to respondents that the type of student in question was assumed to be above average scholastically; the term "English major" was defined as "an A or B liberal arts college graduate with a thorough grounding in composition (including not only freshman English but advanced grammar); with a knowledge of literature ranging from *The Iliad* to the most modern novels; with the ability to set down in a concise, a logical, and an orderly manner materials obtained through research; and, perhaps, with a modicum of creativity." Ordinarily, the student would have taken a minimum of thirty semester hours or forty-five quarter hours of English courses.

It is conceded that considerations other than college background enter into the professional picture, for the degree contributes only partially to the development of the person as a whole. Success, in the final analysis, is a product of rearing, social adjustment, native intelligence, and maturity as well as formal education. Initiative, temperament, tenaciousness, affability, common sense, physical appearance, quality of voice, sense of humor, patience, social consciousness, community interests, and even religious convictions, to name but a few possibilities, may conceivably have a bearing on a person's ability to hold a position, earn promotions, and be content with employment. This study makes no attempt to evaluate the effect of English training on the personality and surely makes no claim that such academic products are all well suited for legal, medical, industrial, or governmental careers. It does indicate, however, that in these four areas, other personal qualifications aside, graduates with this scholastic background have a distinct edge over graduates with other preparations.

English as a Prelaw or Premedical Major

It is surely no secret that for years the majority of college advisers have closely supervised the undergraduate education of prelegal and premedical students and have prescribed for them a regimen of carefully selected courses that are considered to contribute directly to their career preparation. Not infrequently these courses anticipate others that will be taken later at the professional schools. Prelegal programs outlined in college bulletins often recommend multiple courses in political science, history, accounting, public speaking, and law as well as individual courses in business administration, human anatomy, criminology, and even marriage and family life. Lip service is usually paid to the need for future lawyers to be proficient in written and oral expression, but rarely are they specifically advised to major in English. Similarly, premedical students are usually advised to take far more science courses than they actually need to enter medical school, the prinicipal justification being that competition for admission is keen and requires additional advanced preparation. A typical state university, for example, requires of its premedical students sixty-three semester hours of science, yet the state medical school for which these students are being groomed requires for admission only forty-six (which in itself is far above average). To make matters worse, all of this work is crammed into three years to enable students to hurry off to medical school without completing a baccalaureate program. Should they choose to complete the senior year, they are urged to elect additional courses in botany, chemistry, microbiology, or zoology! It is little wonder that a staff member of the state medical school recently complained that his students are sadly lacking in communications skills and experience difficulty in writing case histories.

Yet, a survey of a substantial number of law and medical schools reveals unquestionably that such specialization for undergraduates not only is unnecessary but is actually considered by many to be undesirable. In answer to the question "Is it ordinarily possible for a college undergraduate both to meet your entrance requirements and complete an English major?," all responding forty-five law schools and thirty-one medical schools answered "yes." A review of their entrance requirements explains why.

Admission to law school in no way depends on undergraduate course specialization. One must have, usually, a degree conferred by an accredited four-year institution; a minimum grade-point average—from 2.2 to 2.6 on a four-point scale; and an acceptable score on the Law School Admission Test, which gauges an applicant's fitness to enter the legal profession. A descriptive word regarding the latter may be appropriate to assure those who are unfamiliar with it that no prelaw courses are needed (or even exist, for that matter) to make a satisfactory score. The current LSAT is in seven parts. First, the candidate is given a topic on which to write a clear, logical, succinct, and, of course, accurate essay in thirty minutes. The essay is followed by a Reading Comprehension section consisting of questions about passages on a variety of subjects, an Analytical Reading section requiring the candidate to derive information and deduce relations from sets of conditions, an Evaluation of Facts section challenging the candidate to separate the wheat from the chaff in simple legal disputes, and a Logical Reasoning section testing the candidate's ability to reach sound conclusions from material in a variety of passages. There are two additional sections that vary from year to year but that follow the same general lines as the preceding ones; emphasis is placed consistently on rapid and accurate understanding of written material and the proper application of facts derived therefrom. Obviously, one's best preparation for such a test, for which there is no cramming, is a liberal arts program with a major in English.

Medical college entrance requirements, though not to be underestimated, have been subject to considerable exaggeration. Most medical schools require only thirty-two semester hours of science courses for admission. This is about twenty-one hours more than the average student takes, for at least eleven hours—eight of science and three of mathematics—are required of all students by most institutions. Additional requirements vary, but considerable weight is usually placed on the results of a personal interview with an admissions committee. Many schools, though certainly not all, require a minimum score on the Medical College Admissions Test. The MCAT, often a second justification for an abundance of advanced science courses in premedical curricula, covers four areas: Science Knowledge, Science Problems, Skills Analysis (Reading), and Skills Analysis (Quantitative). The science covered in parts 1 and 2 does not extend beyond introductory undergraduate courses in general biology, chemistry, physics, and organic chemistry; the mathematics does not include calculus. Parts 3 and 4, however, are thorough-going reading examinations that consist of questions on long essays to test not what one already knows but what one can rapidly derive from reading unfamiliar material of various types. In these sections all the necessary facts are contained in the reading passages. Again, as in the case of the LSAT, the advantage of well-rounded liberal arts English majors is evident. Provided, of course, that they are well grounded in mathematics and the sciences, their broader literary experience affords them a definite advantage over colleagues who have restricted themselves to a limited curriculum, studying material that, to a great extent, will be repeated in medical school.

It is clear, then, that students anticipating careers in law and medicine can with little difficulty both qualify for entrance to professional school and major in English. Even with the extra science courses, an English premedical student at a typical liberal arts college can meet all the requirements for graduation and have a margin of from eighteen to twenty-seven hours to spare for electives. But will such students be admitted even though they qualify? All the law and medical schools that participated in the survey answered emphatically in the affirmative: these applicants have been and are being admitted, although medical schools concede that relatively few English majors apply.

The vital question is whether English majors perform well enough at these professional institutions to be considered desirable. On this point the responses were far from discouraging. While thirteen law and twenty medical schools were hesitant to express an opinion that might be interpreted as a preference for one undergraduate major over another (an opinion that the survey questionnaire did not request, by the way), the remaining institutions stated unreservedly that past experience proved such applicants to be highly desirable. The following comments from law schools best indicate the extent of their enthusiasm:

> It can be strenuously argued that a major in literature is one of the best backgrounds for the study and practice of law. Articulation and communication are essential ingredients of the lawyer's professional equipment. At the same time, such a background gives deep insight into human nature. (Camille W. Cook, assistant to the dean, University of Alabama School of Law)

> I majored in English in my A.B. program in preparation for law school. I advised my two sons who are now lawyers to do likewise. None has regretted it. (A. E. Papale, dean, Loyola University School of Law, New Orleans, Louisiana)

> The ability to use the English language effectively is the most important ability an applicant can bring to the study of law, and the lack of this ability is the most frequent cause for failure of law students. I am confident that the same connection between this ability and success will be found in the practice of law. For this reason we recommend a major in English, and we put particular emphasis upon the grades an applicant has earned in English courses. (James C. Quarles, dean, Walter R. George School of Law, Mercer University)

> An English major is considered to be the very best for those who intend to enter law school. (Ernest A. Raba, dean, School of Law, St. Mary's University, San Antonio, Texas)

> In my opinion English probably is the best undergraduate major for most law students, followed by economics and history. Because a lawyer's principal tools are words, a strong background in English and its use gives that student some advantage in law school work. The chief complaint of most legal educators is that most law students are too poorly equipped in our language. (Orley R. Lilly, Jr., chair, Admissions Committee, University of Tulsa College of Law)

Medical school comments sounded the same theme:

> Many of our students come to us well prepared in science but poorly prepared in discourse and writing. Communication is critically important to a physician. Good preparation in English is mandatory; excellent preparation invaluable. (Horace N. Marvin, dean, University of Arkansas School of Medicine)

> Given a basic interest in and aptitude for science, personally I would prefer a non-science major. The "literacy" rate seems to be decreasing—God help us! So the more English majors you give us, the better. (Robert L. Tuttle, dean, Bowman Gray School of Medicine)

> The ability to communicate is of critical importance in medicine, so that a thorough knowledge of the English language and its literature is a valuable asset for a medical student. I teach a course in Medicine in Shakespeare for students here, partly for this reason. (Frank N. Miller, dean, George Washington University School of Medicine)

> We like to have English majors apply to the medical school. I have observed that their communications skills are of considerable benefit to them in medicine. (D. J. Klepper, dean, University of New Mexico School of Medicine)

Nor were the attitudes of the twenty medical schools that declined to state an opinion negative. On the contrary, although they avoided placing emphasis on any one undergraduate area of concentration, they revealed a common interest in good students regardless of major, be it English, history, psychology, drama, foreign languages, or education. The bulletin of the Baylor University College of Medicine summarizes admirably the position of most medical schools:

> The applicant is advised to use the period of college study to gain . . . the beginnings of a broad liberal education in the art of communication; the fundamental principles of science; the history, habits, philosophy, and organization of [modern] society. The applicant may choose for [a] major any subject which seems to offer broad opportunities for the development of intellectual discipline and critical thinking; however, proficiency in the sciences must be demonstrated clearly.

And, finally, the Association of American Medical Colleges itself has added solid backing to this position. After a three-year study, a nineteen-member panel sponsored by the AAMC reported in September 1984 on the continuing and even accelerating "erosion" of general education for physicians; the panel strongly urged remedial measures, including redesigning the MCAT to place less emphasis on biology, chemistry, and physics to prevent "premature specialization and to encourage premedical students to get a broader undergraduate education."

A number of schools, though by no means all, have become aware of this attitude on the part of medical colleges and have either drastically curtailed undergraduate specialization or, as in the case of the University of West Virginia and a few others, have eliminated their premedical programs as such. Bulletin descriptions like the following by George Washington University are becoming more numerous and may be typical in just a few years:

> With the exception of these specific requirements [a total of twenty-four semester hours of science courses], applicants are urged to follow their personal interests in developing their premedical courses of study. A well-balanced program, rather than a specific field, is the criterion by which the applicant is judged. It is not advisable to take courses that appear to cover subject matter in the medical program.

There can be no question, therefore, that liberal arts English majors can qualify for admission to a law or medical school, that they have an excellent chance of being accepted, and that, from the educational viewpoint, they are exceptionally well equipped to succeed. Despite the tendency of many colleges and universities (particularly those that are state-supported) to encourage students to specialize early, professional schools in these two fields are becoming increasingly interested in the applicant who has used undergraduate education to explore various academic areas in an effort to gain a broad exposure to the humanities, a deeper insight into human behavior, and a mind that is trained to think critically and logically, to interpret rapidly and accurately, and to articulate its observations and conclusions with clarity and precision. Not only students but college professors and administrators would do well to keep abreast of this development.

English as a Precommerce Major

Nearly all students who enter college to prepare for a business career are advised to follow a well-defined and highly restricted "business" curriculum, usually under the auspices of a department, school, or college (depending on the size of the institution) of business administration. Once these students have completed a token number of liberal arts courses, including freshman and sophomore English, their program consists solidly of accounting, economics, marketing, finance, and management courses, totaling from sixty to eighty-four semester hours, more than double the hours needed for any liberal arts major. It is expected that the result will be a graduate adequately prepared to enter the world of commerce; and it is usually this student, whose specific training and goals are known to the placement bureaus, who is notified when prospective employers visit the campus.

While it is certainly unjust to disparage the work of college and university schools of business administration, which have performed an important and useful service for both students and industry, it is necessary to point out that employers are voicing dissatisfaction with managerial employees who specialized before they achieved a well-rounded education.

As the *Wall Street Journal* and the *Journal of College Placement* have pointed out, during the past twenty years an alarmingly increasing number of the most promising products of highly reputable business colleges have become "floaters"; unable to hold a position for more than one year, they have drifted from job to job searching for one that really suits them (or at which they can succeed).[3] Although a number of reasons have been advanced to explain this phenomenon, employers themselves point to two factors. First, most of their college-trained employees simply are not literate enough to hold managerial positions or to absorb the requisite training. A training administrator for a large construction-materials corporation notes that although not every employee needs to be "a finished public speaker or writer," all employees need to "be able to com-

municate. . . . Some of the reports that I have had occasion to read over the years would curl your hair, and as for oral presentation—many of them can charitably be called atrocious." The personnel director for one of America's largest insurance firms says, "One of the chief weaknesses of many college graduates is the inability to express themselves well. Even though technically qualified, they will not advance far with such a handicap." An official of an internationally known food-products corporation states, "The ability to read and comprehend what one reads and the ability to translate orally are essential to communication. Communication is essential to controlling and directing people, and people (with the help of machines, but, I repeat, *people*) get the job done! Reading and speaking and people are the ingredients or the raw materials in a business. [An employee] who can use good, plain, understandable English is worth more to me than a specialist." Many companies have resorted to night classes in English and communication as a solution but with limited success. The personnel manager of a financial advisory firm describes as a "lost cause" a candidate who "does not have basic speaking and writing skills at age twenty-one."

Second, it is pointed out that these unsuccessful persons specialized too soon and, consequently, lack the liberal arts foundation that is needed for managerial success. Again, night courses have been utilized in an attempt to fill the gap and have enjoyed little success. But why is such a background necessary? A business executive offers this explanation:

> One of our problems today is a lack of values. Business administration is value-less. Young people need a sound foundation in history, sociology, psychology, mathematics, literature, comparative religion, government, etc., so that they can develop a mature personal philosophy. The failure to provide assistance in this kind of development has led to a proliferation of "Executive Development" programs, which attempt to compensate for this loss with all kinds of sophisticated crash programs years later. Had undergraduate schools done their jobs properly, there would be no markets for "Sensitivity Training" and "Managerial Grids."

The theme is sounded repeatedly by other authoritative voices. Robert E. Beck, assistant vice-president, human relations, AT&T, reported in his 1980 pamphlet *Career Patterns: The Liberal Arts Major in the Bell System Management* the results of a twenty-year study: company employees with liberal arts degrees proved markedly superior in administrative skills, leadership skills, oral communication skills, and forcefulness of personal impact to those with science, engineering, and business degrees. And again, Robert B. Smith, executive vice-president of General Motors, in his 1980 pamphlet *Why Business Needs the Liberal Arts*, observes, "Only leadership with many and varied talents can hope to be successful in such an ideological marketplace—and this is why the liberal arts in industry are assuming so much importance today." He goes on to say that "narrow-visioned" specialists are out of their element in such an environment. And yet again, the May 1985 report of the Business–Higher Education Forum charges that business graduates lack not only adequate skills in writing and oral communication but also sufficient exposure to disciplines outside the business school that would give them "a better appreciation of the complex interrelationships that govern decisions in today's business."

It would seem, therefore, that a liberal arts English major who wishes to pursue a career in private industry is just what many employers are seeking. But is this merely talk, or are such graduates actually being hired by "big business"? If so, are they succeeding? What types of organizations hire them? What careers are open to them? What attributes, other than generally good English, have they derived from their training that industry finds especially desirable? Finally, what courses might these students elect to improve their chances of success in business? A representative segment of private industry has provided significant answers.

When asked, "Do you hire college graduates who have a liberal arts education with a major in English even though they lack special training in your area?, " eighty-five percent of nearly four hundred companies replied "yes." Cutting across the broad spectrum of the business world, these large, highly diversified organizations represented nearly every type of commercial enterprise; classified according to the prinicipal interests of each, they may be arranged in the following twenty-two categories: aircraft, automotive, banking, brewing, chain store, chemical and drug, clothing and textile, communications, construction materials, electrical and electronics, food products, fuel, glass products, household equipment, insurance, machinery and tools, metals, office equipment, paper products, public transportation, publications, and rubber. A few of the names of the organizations that responded will indicate their quality and size: Allis-Chalmers, American Airlines, American Broadcasting Company, Bank of America, Bethlehem Steel, Blue Cross and Blue Shield, Boeing, Borden, General Electric, General Mills, General Motors, General Tire, International Business Machines, Litton Industries, Minnesota Mining and Manufacturing, Proctor and Gamble, Samsonite, Sears and Roebuck, Standard Oil, Westinghouse, and Xerox. And the rest were of this caliber.

To be sure, English graduates have many opportunities for employment outside of the classroom in "literary" fields, but it is indeed a misconception that they are limited to these, as the personnel manager of a major food-products organization pointed out:

We all know the various positions in journalism, radio, television, education, etc., that are generally thought of as being the careers available for English majors. However, the field is very broad indeed, for communication – or lack of communication – is responsible for eight-tenths of all of industry's problems. . . . If these A and B college graduates have the imagination and are willing to accept the challenge, there is no job in management . . . which could not be theirs and in which they could not be of definite service.

More specifically, applicants with a college English background are hired by industry to fill positions in two broad categories. The first utilizes this educational background directly for editing, technical writing, advertising, communications, and other functions requiring grammatical accuracy and literary skills. The other uses the formal education only as an adjunct to the performance of duties in such areas as sales, marketing, personnel management, systems engineering, and programming, positions that require logical thinking and facility in exact communication rather than a specific set of learned skills. It is in the latter category that by far the greater number of employment opportunities arise.

The variety of positions that can be and are held by former English majors is astounding. Personnel managers who were surveyed listed hundreds of positions for which these graduates might qualify, and many not only admitted that they themselves were former English majors but cited friends with the same undergraduate background who are now successful in business. Having furnished such a list, which included two vice-presidents, Edward Mandt, personnel manager for Borden, added:

I could cite many others – none of whom are teaching – which should lay to rest the myth that an English major can expect difficulty in securing a position in other than the teaching profession. Many companies recognize the value of a liberal education. In fact, several have had to send their trained (but not educated) executives back to school in later years in an attempt to acquire it. It is far preferable [to get a] liberal education before the job and technical training on the job or in night school than the other way around.

Prompted by the survey, a number of organizations ran computer checks of their personnel records to ascertain positions currently held by former English majors. The results of three of these are listed in table 1. One was prepared by an aircraft company, one by a manufacturer of office equipment, and one by a steel firm. Each is a division of a larger corporation. It should be observed that while there are a number of writing positions, it is clear that the English major can branch out into a broad range of areas, including computer programming, information and analysis, and management. Additional statistics furnished by the aircraft company regarding its list are also somewhat illuminating. The employees listed ranged in age from twenty-four to fifty-three, and their years with the firm from one (those recently hired at entry-level positions) to eighteen. The relatively even employment distribution during the eighteen-year period indicates a modest but steady availability of jobs for such persons even at this highly technical installation. Eight persons had taken positions with this company on receiving their degrees and had remained—two, thus far, for eighteen years; the others were employed with from three to seventeen years of experience elsewhere, which enabled them to secure positions at "advanced levels." Five of the listed positions were held by women, two who had recently joined the company and three who had served the company eight, fifteen, and eighteen years respectively; their jobs were administrative secretary; public information assistant; administrative associate, engineering; wage and salary representative; and senior mathematician.

Table 2 presents graphically the career areas into which the scores of positions listed by personnel managers may be grouped. Listed vertically on the left are the twenty-two types of organizations that were mentioned earlier, plus a catchall group entitled "Others," which includes categories represented by fewer than four companies (such as tobacco and firearms). The next column shows the number of companies in each category that participated in the survey. Seven career areas are listed horizontally, top right: personnel relations, sales and marketing, public relations, management, advertising, editing and writing, and research and investigation. Tabulated under each are the numbers of individual organizations in each category that noted career opportunities for English majors. For example, in the aircraft industry, eighteen of nineteen companies listed various career opportunities in editing and writing; of twenty-eight chemical and drug firms, seventeen listed opportunities in sales and marketing; and of thirty-two food products organizations, twenty listed opportunities in all seven categories. The average was four areas per company. Personnel relations, well in the lead, was listed by 62% of those participating, followed by sales and marketing, 58%; public relations, 51%; management, 50%; advertising, 44%; editing and writing,

43%; and research and investigation, 22%.

Yet it must be observed that, in order to ascertain the views of a representative cross section of private industry, deliberate precautions were taken not to weight this survey in favor of applicants with literary training and interests. These figures, therefore, although they reveal a preponderance of administrative, sales, and advertising positions, should not be construed to mean that writing and editing opportunities are rare. On the contrary, as Charles B. Stoll, vice-president of John Wiley and Sons, observed in a recent publication, the mammoth book-publishing industry offers a wealth of such positions to English majors, who may serve as sponsoring or subject editors, editorial supervisors, copy editors, "depth" editors, picture editors, editorial assistants, and editorial secretaries, as well as specialists who develop programmed and audiovisual instruction materials and techniques of educational testing—*all in addition to* managerial and sales positions.[4] For a detailed discussion of such opportunities, see "Writing-Related Careers" below.

A question naturally arises at this point: what traits does a college-trained English major have that the business world judges desirable? The same business executives who furnished the above information answered this question as well.

First, it was agreed generally that the following are abilities of an English major that are useful in commercial employment (although no one person could be expected to have them all):

1. To speak well in public.
2. To handle office paperwork with grammatical accuracy, conciseness, and clarity.
3. To edit or rewrite material that has been prepared by technical personnel.

Table 1. Positions Currently Held by Former English Majors
Now Employed by Divisions of Three Large Corporations

[Aircraft]

administrative analyst, engineering
administrative analyst, logistic support
administrative associate, engineering
administrative secretary
buyer
data-processing programmer
editing, publications group supervisor
engineering information analyst
methods analyst
public information assistant
scientific information assistant
senior accountant
senior administrative associate
senior aircraft service manuals engineer
senior aircraft structures engineer
senior mathematician
senior production liaison engineer
technical librarian
wage and salary representative

[Office Equipment]

associate industrial engineer
associate programmer
associate writer
buyer
distribution staff aid
manager, communication services
manager, process systems
manager, production services
manager, sales administration
manager, systems center
market data analyst
packaging engineer
professional employment representative
project designer
senior business development analyst
senior copywriter
senior engineer
senior market application analyst
systems analyst
teleprocessing analyst

[Steel]

advertising trainee
area inspection foreman
assistant to works manager
audiovisual adviser
catalog reference librarian
director, personnel planning and development
dispatcher
editor
employment interviewer
expediter, purchasing
general manager, products
metallurgical assistant
personnel adviser
programmer
senior technical representative
service correspondent
supervisor, claims
time study consultant

8

Type of organization	Number reporting	Personnel relations	Sales and marketing	Public relations	Management	Advertising	Editing and writing	Research and investigation
Aircraft	19	16	8	17	8	12	18	4
Automotive	7	6	3	6	2	4	1	3
Banking	9	7	0	4	7	0	6	6
Brewing	4	1	4	3	2	3	1	0
Chain store	9	4	4	3	6	3	1	1
Chemical and drug	28	19	17	15	15	15	14	5
Clothing and textile	10	6	9	2	8	3	2	3
Communications	12	8	8	7	10	3	5	3
Construction materials	6	5	5	1	4	3	3	1
Electrical and electronics	15	9	6	8	5	8	9	1
Food products	32	20	19	9	20	14	8	1
Fuel	16	8	11	6	4	5	2	2
Glass products	7	4	6	5	4	4	2	1
Household equipment	7	5	6	5	5	7	3	1
Insurance	34	22	23	23	26	15	15	13
Machinery and tools	8	6	5	2	4	3	1	1
Metals	21	11	8	10	6	5	2	2
Office equipment	18	10	12	13	7	10	13	3
Paper products	13	9	11	5	3	4	1	1
Public transportation	6	4	2	2	3	2	3	4
Publishing	16	4	8	6	3	8	15	8
Rubber	4	3	4	3	2	2	3	0
Others	21	14	8	11	10	8	10	7
Totals	322	201	187	166	164	141	138	71
Percentages		62%	58%	51%	50%	44%	43%	22%

4. To analyze, interpret, reorganize, and rephrase material.
5. To use general and specialized reference materials in preparing well-documented reports.
6. To analyze and interpret unpublished data of various kinds in preparing well-documented reports.
7. To use research materials with creativity and originality.
8. To speak and write a foreign language fluently.
9. To become reasonably knowledgeable in areas in which there has been no previous training.
10. To present an argument or to debate logically, succinctly, and clearly.

Next, the respondents were asked to evaluate each of these items as to its importance. Table 3 shows the statistical results.[5] It should first be pointed out that the standing of the last two items is not completely indicative of their commercial value. Foreign language proficiency is tenth primarily because ninety percent of the installations of the represented firms are located in the continental United States; nevertheless, a few companies with large international interests (particularly in the chemical, household equipment, and communications fields) consider it of first importance. Similarly, although "technical writing" (no. 9) was ranked very high by a number of aircraft, automotive, and office equipment firms, these companies represented only one-eighth of those reporting.

While being able to handle paperwork with accuracy,

Table 3. Abilities of English Majors, Rated by Companies as to First, Second, or Third Importance

Type of organization	To become knowledge-able in previously unfamiliar areas	To analyze, interpret, reorganize, rephrase material	To present an argument logically, succinctly, clearly	To speak well in public	To prepare well-documented reports, type B*	To prepare well-documented reports, type A*	To use research materials with originality	To handle paperwork with accuracy and clarity	To edit or rewrite material prepared by technical personnel	To write and speak a foreign language
Aircraft	1.53	1.25	1.67	1.77	1.74	1.76	1.89	1.50	1.41	2.94
Automotive	1.67	1.33	1.72	1.86	1.83	1.50	1.67	1.72	1.17	3.00
Banking	1.67	1.13	1.67	1.88	1.67	1.33	1.33	1.88	2.17	3.00
Brewing	1.67	1.33	1.67	1.67	1.67	1.67	2.33	2.00	2.00	3.00
Chain store	1.00	1.70	1.70	1.50	2.00	2.50	2.50	1.70	2.50	3.00
Chemical and drug	1.21	1.50	1.94	1.64	1.68	1.93	1.50	2.11	1.87	2.81
Clothing and textile	1.27	1.64	1.36	1.40	1.70	1.80	1.80	1.70	1.90	3.00
Communications	1.29	1.73	1.60	1.85	1.86	2.42	1.92	1.67	2.42	2.83
Construction materials	2.00	1.50	1.75	2.00	1.60	1.60	2.25	2.25	1.75	3.00
Electrical and electronics	1.36	1.61	1.45	1.36	2.00	1.72	1.72	1.72	1.50	2.90
Food products	1.15	1.73	1.42	1.42	1.69	2.08	1.87	2.08	2.33	2.87
Fuel	1.40	1.37	1.33	1.22	1.50	2.10	2.00	1.77	2.50	2.87
Glass products	1.16	1.57	1.25	1.75	2.00	2.00	2.00	2.00	2.50	3.00
Household equipment	1.00	1.66	1.00	1.00	1.20	1.33	1.80	2.20	2.00	2.33
Insurance	1.20	1.52	1.46	1.66	1.65	1.87	1.79	1.85	1.78	2.90
Machinery and tools	1.50	1.50	1.75	1.00	1.66	2.00	2.50	1.75	2.66	3.00
Metals	1.44	1.28	1.53	1.69	1.84	1.61	1.76	1.92	1.76	2.84
Office equipment	1.27	1.17	1.53	1.66	1.50	1.82	1.53	2.01	1.44	2.92
Paper products	1.43	1.60	1.43	1.40	2.00	2.22	2.40	2.20	2.00	3.00
Public transportation	1.60	1.40	1.60	2.00	2.25	2.00	1.75	1.75	1.50	3.00
Publishing	1.53	1.00	2.50	2.57	2.00	1.60	1.21	1.66	1.37	2.85
Rubber	1.00	1.66	1.00	1.33	1.33	1.33	1.33	2.00	1.66	3.00
Others	1.11	1.12	1.88	1.33	1.25	1.50	1.50	1.77	2.55	3.00
Overall averages	1.37	1.45	1.54	1.62	1.76	1.78	1.84	1.86	1.90	2.90

*Type A: reports based on general and specialized reference materials.

conciseness, and clarity is generally conceded to be a valuable asset, it is a skill that most companies expect of *every* employee who is placed in a position of responsibility and therefore ranks no higher than eighth in this list of desirable attributes of the English major. Rated slightly higher is the ability to use research materials with creativity and originality. Of still greater value is the more specialized skill of preparing well-documented reports (nos. 5 and 6), a skill that is developed to a great extent by the writing of "research papers," which are often challenged in educational circles as useful only to those contemplating academic careers. Next in importance are the twin traits of being able to speak well in public and being logical and effective in debate; and next above those is the ability to analyze, interpret, reorganize, and rephrase written materials, tasks that constantly confront the administrator. Above all is that which was assigned first importance by two-thirds of the respondents: the ability to cope successfully with previously unfamiliar subject matter, or, to put it more simply, the ability to continue to learn. That this trait is especially characteristic of good English majors has long been recognized by experienced professors and, it seems, has not escaped the attention of employers. This, says James P. Pilkington, Director of Personnel, Methodist Publishing House, is the "greatest asset of an English major," who, he adds, has the "flexibility and adaptability to different types of work and different types of situations."

In short, it should be of considerable comfort to English professors to know that the emphasis they place on written and oral accuracy, on clear and logical organization in shorter compositions, on the gathering of information through research, on the careful organization and documentation of written reports, on comprehending, interpreting, and analyzing literary material, and on rewriting to achieve more effective expression is hardly misplaced; and numerous letters and notes supplementing the above information underscored this point. Typical of these are the remarks of William Austin, president of Gaffers and Sattler, Incorporated, a subsidiary of Magic Chef:

> To sum up, a successful executive should be able effectively to analyze and interpret information . . . and most important, be able to [communicate] effectively. A solid background in English grammar, composition, and literature is a great help in developing these abilities.

Nor is the type of student who makes As and Bs not only in literature but in all college courses merely an academic drudge; rather, it is this student who has the intellectual capacity, the mental discipline, and the interest catholicity that big business especially prizes. And the reason is obvious. Few college graduates are adequately trained for their jobs when companies first risk hiring them.[6] Unless the employees have the capacity to learn, to be trained, they are of no use; further, unless they can adapt themselves to changing situations such as transfers from one phase of a company's operation to another, their hopes of future promotion are badly jeopardized and the likelihood of their joining the ranks of the "floaters" greatly increased.

Looking beyond these attributes, a number of business executives observed that the study of literature contributes something else that not only enables English majors to compete with business administration majors for managerial positions but gives them a distinct advantage: a basic understanding of human nature, essential in making sound managerial decisions. Richard Hankinson, personnel director of Blue Cross–Blue Shield of Iowa, wrote at length on this point, astutely observing that

> Understanding is convertible to action and understanding requires almost "gut" level feeling. How do you teach this to managers? I think that one answer lies within literature, for literature is the only vicarious source of the feeling and understanding that comes through identification and introspection.

And he added this intriguing note:

> Sometime, in the not too distant future, we are going to experiment with a course in management development based on literature. I can't help feeling that any individual who is capable of dealing with Anderson's concept of the "grotesque" in *Winesburg, Ohio* or who is capable of understanding the source of desperation in Willie Loman and the course of his ultimate destruction will be more effective. Too many times our managers understand only the theoretical basis of behavior without understanding the way it may affect the individual. I think the study of literature may overcome some of this handicap.

Similarly, Harris Shane, vice-president of Pullman, Incorporated, commented:

> The study of literature is the study of human behavior. One can look upon some novels as case studies. I recall pondering at some length on the question raised in *Arrival and Departure* of whether motivation should be evaluated in judging a person who has behaved superbly. The English major has probably done more thinking about why people act as they do than a major in any other subject.

To assist in counseling English students who have an eye to a future in business, the companies participating in the survey were requested to check any of fourteen listed courses that they considered beneficial as electives and to add any others that occurred to them as important. The results are presented in table 4.

This table is like table 2 except that course titles have taken the place of career areas. As one can see at a glance, there is no hint of unanimity, primarily because of the differences in operational requirements of the various companies. Regardless of these variations, which students might

Table 4. Suggested Electives for English Majors Anticipating Business Careers

Type of organization	Number reporting	Electives													
		Principles of management	Introduction to economics	Human relations	General psychology	Principles of accounting	Personnel management	Industrial management	Industrial psychology	Technical writing	Public address	Business law	Psychology of personality	Typing	Bookkeeping
Aircraft	19	15	11	12	7	9	12	9	6	17	7	11	4	3	3
Automotive	7	6	5	6	4	5	4	5	5	3	2	3	4	4	3
Banking	9	7	8	5	3	9	4	2	1	2	1	4	0	0	0
Brewing	4	3	3	3	3	2	1	2	2	1	2	3	1	2	0
Chain store	9	9	7	8	4	4	6	3	2	2	5	3	1	2	2
Chemical and drug	28	21	13	15	20	16	14	14	12	12	8	8	8	5	1
Clothing and textile	10	7	5	6	3	2	3	3	4	1	3	3	4	2	1
Communications	12	8	8	5	3	8	5	4	3	1	2	2	4	3	2
Construction materials	6	3	4	2	3	4	1	2	2	2	1	2	1	0	0
Electrical and electronics	15	9	8	9	7	6	6	7	4	9	6	3	3	4	1
Food products	32	26	23	19	17	17	11	12	12	5	11	10	11	2	2
Fuel	16	13	12	8	7	8	5	4	5	4	9	10	2	2	1
Glass products	7	4	6	2	3	3	3	2	5	1	2	0	1	1	0
Household equipment	7	6	5	4	4	5	3	3	2	3	1	2	3	1	0
Insurance	34	30	25	25	18	18	10	7	13	5	12	16	12	6	2
Machinery and tools	8	5	3	5	3	3	6	5	7	2	4	1	2	1	0
Metals	21	13	11	9	10	8	11	9	11	8	6	7	6	2	1
Office equipment	18	11	10	8	4	7	5	8	4	10	3	2	2	3	1
Paper products	13	10	9	9	8	6	6	7	7	4	7	7	5	0	1
Public transportation	6	3	3	3	3	3	3	2	2	2	1	0	1	0	1
Publishing	16	5	4	5	10	2	3	2	0	7	3	1	1	10	0
Rubber	4	2	2	2	1	1	1	2	3	3	2	1	3	1	0
Others	21	9	7	6	7	5	6	3	4	3	6	4	3	1	0
Totals	322	225	192	176	152	151	129	117	116	107	104	103	82	55	20
Percentages		70%	60%	55%	47%	47%	40%	36%	36%	33%	32%	32%	25%	17%	6%

heed if they knew the specific type of business for which they were preparing, the overall trend is quite clear. Seventy percent of all those reporting chose Principles of Management, 60% Introduction to Economics, 55% Human Relations, 47% General Psychology (which most liberal arts students take anyway), and 47% Principles of Accounting. These five seem generally to be most advisable, and fortunately they usually have no prerequisites. The next course, Personnel Management, checked by 40%, would obviously have its advantages, too, considering the large number of personnel opportunities noted by the companies. But regardless of the student's choices, it would not be advisable to infringe on a liberal arts education by taking more than six such electives. Five was the average number recommended by the companies, and not a few advocated no courses at all beyond those in liberal arts.

These are encouraging comments, facts, and figures, indeed, but a word of caution is due. Although liberal arts English majors are a desirable commodity, it is presently unrealistic for them to expect to be hotly pursued by campus recruiters with contracts in hand. Rather, it is the applicants who must be the aggressors, and they should not wait until after graduation to begin to act. In a college that has a placement office, as most do, students should begin their job-hunting campaign by filing with it no later than the fall of the senior year. It is true that many campus recruiters have in mind persons of specialized training, such as accountants, scientists, and engineers, but there are also plenty who seek good applicants regardless of course concentration and are glad to interview promising English majors. These opportunities, of course, are of no avail to the student who is not aware of them or who has not completed a placement office dossier for a recruiter to peruse prior to an interview. The following procedure may be helpful as a guide.

1. Students should, early in the senior year, file with the college or university placement office and, following its guidelines, complete a dossier as carefully as possible. Special care should be given to the choice of references, and each should be told the type of employment that is being sought. References for a teaching position differ markedly from those needed for a job in private industry.

2. They should keep posted regarding scheduled visits of company representatives, who usually indicate in advance the type of applicant they are seeking. Students should note those who do not specify a particular major area and request interviews with as many of these as possible. Interviewing experience is valuable, and one can always turn down an offer that one does not want.

3. Prior to an interview, students should prime themselves with as much information as they can obtain about the company: its size, products, diversification, plant locations, growth possibilities, business reputation, and organization. There are some good books to consult for this and even more information. One that the placement office itself will probably have is the official directory of the regional placement associations, *College Placement Annual*. Two others are available in most libraries: *Moody's Handbook of Common Stocks*, a quick reference source for background and statistics on more than 2,300 industries; and *Moody's Industrial Manual*, which provides a comprehensive analysis of every industrial firm listed on the New York and American Stock Exchanges, plus some unlisted companies. Both books are published by Moody's Investors Service, Inc., 99 Church St., New York, NY 10007.

4. Students should also be prepared to answer personal questions. Particularly, they should be able to review in a concise, orderly, and unhesitating manner their college education, work experience, interests, and abilities. Most of this information will, of course, be in the dossier, but the interviewer, for a number of reasons, may want to hear it from the applicant.

5. During the interview, students should make every effort to present themselves to the best advantage. The recruiter is looking for an adult employee whose words, appearance, and behavior will be advantageous to the firm, not for a sleepy-eyed, straggly-haired, blue-jeaned, gum-chewing slouch. Interviews last about thirty minutes, as a rule; in that brief time applicants must concentrate on communicating with ease and confidence, in action as well as with words, their most favorable points.

The cause is hardly lost if the services of the placement office fail to produce employment. By consulting the reference works mentioned above (particularly those published by Moody's Investors Service), students can learn the headquarters and division addresses of nearly any company in which they may be interested. A carefully worded and neatly typed request for an interview addressed to the personnel manager will usually bring results. To be sure, this approach requires a bit of courage and perseverance, but without these a person should not attempt a business career anyway.

English as a Pre–Federal Service Major

Unquestionably, the United States government ranks as this nation's number one employer. Its work force of nearly three million persons operates on an annual budget that towers four and one-half times above the *total assets* of the country's largest private corporation. Yearly, 300,000 persons are hired merely to replace those who die, retire, or leave the service for other reasons. It is also the most complex of this nation's organizations and the most extensive in operational range, offering countless types of services to a myriad of localities both here and abroad and including virtually every type of occupation found in private industry. And there are plenty of opportunities for college English majors, as this statement by an official of the Department of the Navy indicates: "The number of specific jobs within this department which are susceptible to entry with a background in English . . . is too numerous either to catalogue or describe."

To illustrate, more than ninety installations of governmental agencies are listed within the San Francisco area. Among those represented are the Army, the Air Force, the Marine Corps, the Navy, the Bureau of Mines, the Bureau of Land Management, the Commerce Department, the Federal Deposit Insurance Corporation, the Food and Drug Administration, the Forest Service, the Department of Health and Human Services, the Department of Housing and Urban Development, the Internal Revenue Service, the Labor Department, the National Park Service, the Public Health Service, the Social Security Administration, and the Veterans Administration—the ultimate in diversification! Nevertheless, and this is the point, nearly all these locations, according to civil service records, have positions for which English majors may qualify. Why? John Kadow, assistant postmaster general, management information, speaks for the majority of federal administrators:

> I appreciate that in many technical areas formal training is of help. In scientific areas it is, of course, essential. Nevertheless, I have always firmly believed that the main objective of formal education of a general and business nature should be to round an individual, and teach [him or her] to think, analyze, and, of course, respond intelligently. With these attributes well honed, assuming diligent application, I feel [a person] can pick up the vast majority of specialized knowledge.

A recent survey, similar to that of private industry discussed above, substantiates further that government is indeed a promising field for interested and energetic job-seeking English majors. To begin with, of the fifty-one agencies queried, forty-three (84%) replied—a most gratifying response, as anyone who has conducted a survey by means of mailed questionnaires will agree. In answer to the question, "Are English majors hired by your governmental organization even though they lack special training in your area?," thirty-eight (88%!) replied "yes." These included nine of the eleven executive departments (and branches, such as the Army and the Navy);[7] the Library of Congress; the Government Printing Office; and such independent agencies as Action, the Federal Reserve System, the Environmental Protection Agency, the Equal Employment Opportunities Commission, the Federal Communications Commission, the General Services Administration, the National Foundation on the Arts and Humanities, the Railroad Retirement Board, the Small Business Administration, the United States Postal Service, and the Veterans Administration. Negative answers came from only five, most of which, like the Atomic Energy Commission, are highly specialized. Even more significantly, whereas those answering negatively represent but three-tenths of one percent of the total federal civilian work force, the agencies replying "yes" represent well over eighty percent.

As in private industry, English majors have two career avenues open to them in the federal service. They may qualify for teaching, writing, editorial, and information-services positions that utilize their literary skills and interests directly and almost exclusively; or they may use their education as a broad and substantial foundation on which to build a future in other types of work, chiefly administrative. Although many English majors are hired for the former, most of them flow into the latter and find the results to be amply rewarding.

Although a complete catalog of federal positions for which English majors might reasonably qualify would be difficult to compile, the list that follows, based on the information submitted by agencies on their returned questionnaires, is indicative of what persons with such an educational preparation can do and have done. These positions, the titles of which are not always suitably descriptive, are mostly in the GS-5 and GS-7 range at entry level. The majority were listed by more than one agency (some by as many as a dozen), and most carry the additional term "trainee."

adjudication specialist (claims examiner)
administrative assistant
air traffic controller
alcohol and tobacco tax investigator
border patrol agent
broadcast analyst
budget specialist
building management specialist
computer operator
computer programmer
consular officer
contract specialist
distribution facilities specialist
editorial assistant
educational specialist
employee development specialist
equal employment investigator conciliator
equal employment opportunities specialist
financial management specialist
foreign service officer
general administrator
general assistant
highway safety management specialist
legislative affairs specialist
management analyst
management intern
medical administrative specialist
personnel management specialist
position classification specialist
printing assistant
procurement specialist
program analyst
program specialist
public affairs officer
public information specialist
realty specialist

regional representative
research assistant
revenue officer
social insurance representative
supply management specialist
systems analyst
technical information specialist
transportation industry analyst
treasury enforcement agent
writer-editor

More detailed information about several of these is included in the job-description section that concludes this pamphlet.

As in that of private industry, the survey also afforded respondents an opportunity to comment on the attributes of the English major and to rank them in order of importance. The suggested list was the same as the one given private industry, excepting minor editorial changes. Respondents were requested to rate each item using a one-to-ten scale, *one* signifying "of very little importance" and *ten* "of greatest importance." The results are tabulated below.

Attribute	Average Numerical Rating
Ability to continue to learn or to be trained	9.08
Ability to analyze, interpret, reorganize, and rephrase material	8.44
Ability to handle paperwork with grammatical accuracy, conciseness, and clarity	8.36
Ability to prepare well-documented reports	7.88
Ability to edit or rewrite material that has been prepared by technical personnel	6.92
Ability to present an argument or to debate logically, succinctly, and clearly	6.20
Originality and creativity in making use of research materials	6.16
Ability to speak well in public	5.35
Proficiency in a language other than English	2.40

Inasmuch as most government jobs require training and often carry the designation "trainee" or "intern" at the entry level, it is hardly surprising that the "ability to continue to learn or to be trained" appears solidly on top, as it did in the private industry survey. In fact, in *both* surveys the proportion of the respondents who assigned it the highest rating was two-thirds. And, again echoing the earlier survey, the government respondents recognized the "ability to analyze, interpret, reorganize, and rephrase material" as the second most desirable quality. But then, unlike the representatives of private industry, who reflected

their basic sales and marketing interests in placing public speaking and debating among the top four items, government employers continued to emphasize writing skills, naming as the next three attributes the "ability to handle paperwork with grammatical accuracy, conciseness, and clarity," the "ability to prepare well-documented reports," and the "ability to edit or rewrite material that has been prepared by technical personnel." Thus, the first five items are those that treat writing ability, and, obviously, the more highly developed that ability, the better. The two attributes of oral presentation follow in sixth and eighth positions, although both are still well above the midway point of five in numerical rating; and between them (no. 7) is "originality and creativity in making use of research materials." Last is foreign language proficiency, although the State Department rates language proficiency "10," and other agencies, such as the Department of Defense, the Maritime Commission, and the Federal Reserve System, strongly encourage mastery of "any current foreign language."

Government respondents were additionally given an opportunity to indicate which of these attributes they observed English majors most frequently either to possess or to lack. Although remarks on the negative side were few and inconclusive, there was a readily discernible agreement regarding those attributes most often possessed: (1) the ability to continue to learn or to be trained; (2) the ability to analyze, interpret, reorganize, and rephrase material; and (3) the ability to handle paperwork with grammatical accuracy, conciseness, and clarity—the three that had been rated as the most important!

Clearly, federal employers, like their counterparts in private industry, have a well-defined preference for applicants who can write English in a clear, concise, logical, and interesting manner, who have oral mastery of the language, and, above all, who have the capacity to absorb quickly, understand, and retain additional instruction. And they have observed that English majors meet these requirements especially well.

For counseling purposes, the agencies were requested to check four of the areas listed below in which they believed the English major would do well to take two or three courses in order to prepare further for government service:

accounting	history
biology	journalism
chemistry	management
computer science	mathematics
economics	philosophy
finance	physics
foreign language (to be named if checked)	political science
	psychology
geography	sociology

Of these seventeen areas, only two were unchecked: chemistry and physics. Assuming that the English major would have a strong liberal arts program, the majority recommended electives in these areas outside of the humanities: management, economics, computer science, and finance. Management outdistanced the others by nearly a two-to-one ratio, underscoring the point that many English majors have good administrative futures if they want them.

Current listings of federal job opportunities are available at local state employment service offices and at Federal Job Information Centers (FJICs) of the United States Office of Personnel Management (OPM) (see appendix A for addresses). Although most federal government positions are filled competitively through the OPM or an authorized agency under its direction, some federal organizations fill their vacancies through their own hiring systems. These organizations, which should be approached directly for employment information, are the following:

Defense Intelligence Agency
Civilian Personnel Operations Division
Pentagon
Washington, DC 20301

Federal Bureau of Investigation
10th St. and Pennsylvania Ave. NW
Washington, DC 20535

Federal Reserve System, Board of Governors
20th St. and Constitution Ave. NW
Washington, DC 20551

General Accounting Office
Room 4650
441 G St. NW
Washington, DC 20548

International Development Cooperation Agency
320 21st St. NW
Washington, DC 20523

National Security Agency
Fort Meade, MD 20775

US Nuclear Regulatory Commission
Division of Organization of Personnel
Personnel Resources and Employment Programs Branch
Washington, DC 20555

Postal Rate Commission
Administrative Office, Room 500
2000 L St. NW
Washington, DC 20268

US Postal Service
(Write to local postmaster.)

Tennessee Valley Authority
Division of Personnel
Chief, Employment Branch
Knoxville, TN 37902

United States Mission to the United Nations
799 United Nations Plaza
New York, NY 10017

Veterans Administration, Department of Medicine
  and Surgery

(Send inquiries to Veterans Administration Centers nationwide. Most vacancies are for medically trained personnel.)

Judicial Branch of the Government (except the administ tive office of the United States Courts and the United States Customs Courts)
(Apply to the office listing the position.)

Legislative Branch of the Government (including senators' offices, representatives' offices, the Library of Congress, and the Capitol, but not the Government Printing Office)
(Apply to the office listing the position.)

Applications for positions that are under the examining authority of the OPM may be obtained by writing or visiting the nearest FJIC. For some positions an "assembled examination," or formal written test, is required, but for 85% of the jobs in the competitive service, the applicant's qualifications are judged on the basis of an "unassembled examination," that is, the application package that is submitted.

When filling out *any* government application forms, and particularly these forms on which the applicant's evaluation will be based, one cannot possibly be too painstaking. Carelessly penciled scrawls, illegibility, ignored blanks or questions, dirty smudges, wrinkled or torn sheets, misspelled words, crossed-out comments, light typewriter ribbons, sloppy corrections, or badly reproduced supporting documents can only adversely influence those who receive them. The successful applicant for federal employment must begin with meticulous execution of the necessary forms.

The OPM area office to which the forms are sent evaluates the material and in four to six weeks sends the applicant a notice of results indicating eligibility status and rating score or ineligibility rating. Eligible applicants are listed on a register according to score (including veterans' preference), and the names from the top of the register in rating order are certified to agencies with vacancies to fill. As those at the top of the list are hired, those with lower ratings move up the register.

Although the federal government has periodically revised its employment procedures for civil service positions, it has consistently required successful applicants to have a good command of English. A written standard test that was used several years ago was described as follows in *Supplement to Announcement No. 410:*

> We include questions in this examination to test your knowledge of English usage because ability to communicate clearly is one of the job requirements of all positions under this examination. Employees in administrative, professional, and technical jobs prepare reports, issue instructions, and write letters. The public probably knows the Federal Government best through reports and directives issued by its agencies. When writing such materials, employees must be able to state their message in good English. . . . Questions testing your ability to understand what you have read are included in this test because this ability is essential in carrying out the duties of administrative, professional, and technical jobs. To do such jobs, employees must be able to read and interpret Government manuals and carry out various assignments in accordance with them.

This examination was replaced by the Professional Administrative Career Examination (PACE), of which *Announcement No. 429* said,

> Many federal jobs require the ability to analyze, understand, and interpret written material of varying levels of complexity and to retain the content for at least a limited period of time. Question-type I is primarily designed to test these comprehension and retention abilities. . . . Many federal jobs require the use of clear and succinct verbal and written expression. Basic vocabulary limitations impede the precise correspondence of words and concepts and thus hinder effective language communication.

Although the PACE has now been replaced by an "unassembled" examination, a regional OPM director makes it clear that the emphasis on good English remains unchanged:

> Clear and lucid oral and written skills are always in demand within the Federal service. The rating process for those positions not requiring a written test is based primarily upon a review of the applicant's description of education and experience and comparison to qualification requirements. An applicant who is skilled in organizing and communicating complete and thoroughly described information regarding his/her experience assists in the rating process by facilitating complete crediting and consideration of all appropriate education and experience.

College graduates with a good record are given further incentive to consider federal employment, for they may qualify for a GS-7 position instead of the usual entry-level GS-5, an annual advantage of more than $3,000. To qualify, the applicant must have one of the following:

1. standing in the upper third of the class based on completed college work at the time of application.
2. college grade average of B (2.90 of a possible 4.00) or better. This is either the average of all completed courses or the average of all college courses completed during the last two years of undergraduate work.
3. college grade average of B+ (3.5 of a possible 4.00) or better in the major field, where this field is fully qualifying and directly applicable to the specialty field of the position to be filled. This is either the average of all courses in the major field or the average of courses in the major field completed during the last two years of the undergraduate curriculum.
4. membership in one of the national honor societies. For a complete list, see appendix B.

These opportunities are not limited to those with baccalaureate degrees; English majors with graduate degrees may well qualify for mid-level positions, Grades GS-9 through GS-13, on the basis of their graduate education and teaching, writing, editing, supervisory, and administrative experience. Information regarding these positions as well as the forms with which to apply may be obtained from one of the OPM Federal Job Information Centers.

Oddly enough, it seems that this wealth of opportunity is generally neglected by college and university graduates. A Washington official comments, "I am convinced that no employer offering so much in the way of opportunity has been as overlooked as the Federal Government." A review of the library records of a large state university reveals that reference works on federal employment have been checked out by only four students in two years, and available statistics show that fewer than one percent of the graduating English majors take the trouble to apply. Yet federal jobs many and varied await the student of the humanities, particularly the English major—even during periods of frozen appropriations and budgetary reductions—and it takes but a little effort to discover them.

Writing-Related Careers

There are a remarkable number of jobs in industry and government on which those with English baccalaureate and master's degrees who are well equipped to edit, write, and rewrite may set their sights. These jobs may be divided into two major groups, publications and general business writing, with many subdivisions under each.

Publications is a large and promising area, one that is particularly appealing to English majors with pronounced journalistic interest, aptitudes, and experience. The huge book-publishing industry alone offers a wealth of positions, such as sponsoring or subject editor, editorial supervisor, copy editor, "depth" editor, picture editor, editorial assistant, and editorial secretary, as well as readers of various types and specialists who develop programmed and audiovisual instruction materials and techniques of educational testing. Job descriptions for many of these positions are included below under "Representative Job Descriptions."

Next, there are corporate publications of many kinds. One such publication is the house magazine, published for a company's clientele. Anyone who has purchased even a little bit of stock in a major corporation or bought a new car has surely been placed on a mailing list to receive one of these. How many are there? The *Gebbie House Directory* estimates over fifty thousand, each with a circulation ranging from five to ten thousand.

There are numerous in-house publications for the benefit of employees. Some of these, like Allis-Chalmers's *Scope, Dialog,* and *Focus* and Borden's *Borden Today* and *Borden in the News,* are as elaborate as regular house magazines; others are simply newsletters. Farmer's Insurance Group, for example, has not only a publications editor in charge of producing an in-house magazine but also a sales publications specialist in charge of publishing a *Sales Newsletter* and a claims publications specialist in charge of publishing a *Claims Newsletter,* each with a staff of assistants.

In-house newsletters and bulletins are only a step away from the area of public relations, a field rich in career possibilities for the more adventurous, creative young writers.

Under such position titles as press relations assistant, public relations writer, public relations manager, public relations director, news writer, and communications specialist, they manage, edit, and sometimes rewrite free-lance assignments; write and distribute news releases; and write and edit feature stories on such topics as successful customers, company research, and new products. They also respond to media requests for information, write speeches for their superiors, and organize public relations campaigns and special projects. The attractiveness of these positions will depend, of course, on where the company is located and the scope of its activities. In Los Angeles there is, for example, a much envied person whose job description, public relations and publicity coordinator, reads like this:

- Prepares and directs dissemination of newspaper, radio, and tv press releases for Topper Club activities.
- Provides media and Agency Force publicity for the Portland Rose Festival and assists in the selection of a float theme.
- Coordinates Tournament of Roses activities, including float theme and design, supervision of construction, and dinner for tournament officials, and arranges for all publicity and photography associated with the event.
- Organizes and coordinates Rose Parade Queen contest, including the preparation of all publicity and promotional material, and is responsible for all the queen's activities during parade week.

While the aim of public relations is to create an attractive corporate image, to develop a favorable attitude on the part of the general public toward a given company or industry, the goal of advertising is simply to increase sales. Many firms turn the job over to advertising agencies, which, by the way, themselves hire a great many creative and imaginative writers. But others handle their own advertising, sometimes in conjunction with public relations and sometimes through a separate division. General Electric separates the two functions, having an A&SPO (Advertising and Sales Promotion Operation) as well as a CPRO (Corporate Public Relations Operation). The A&SPO employs over four hundred people, two-thirds of whom are writers who either majored in English or journalism in college or whose extracurricular college activities included working on the newspaper, on the yearbook, or with radio or TV. They hold such positions as advertising copywriter, audiovisual producer, publication writer, publications editor, product publicity writer, and speech writer. A GE executive comments, "They master the subtleties of their specific assignments during a stint on the Advertising and Public Relations training program. . . . What we expect of them fresh out of college is the ability to write with clarity and directness and to know how to plan and organize information to meet a specific business objective." Again, job descriptions for several of these positions are included below.

And then there are hundreds of miscellaneous publications, depending on the company. There are wholesale, retail, and mail-order catalogs; there are myriads of brochures, directories, cookbooks, guidance and promotional directives, employee information bulletins, handbooks, and procedural manuals. And, finally, let us not forget those masterpieces of meticulous writing and editing, the quarterly and annual reports to the stockholders. People, not computers, produce all these kinds of publications.

The second major category is that of general business writing. Under this heading one thinks first, of course, of technical writing. Technical writers are hired by a wide variety of firms, work with countless types of materials, and carry numerous designations, such as technical writer–field service, technical writer–marketing, and so on. Technical writers usually edit and rewrite technical, scientific, or specialized subject matter to render it intelligible and useful to the general reader. They must become familiar with pertinent specialized terminology and be able to determine when information furnished them is inadequate or misleading. They must be able to organize and present information in a clear and concise manner, maintaining established editorial standards and conforming to company, customer, and (in some instances) military or governmental specifications.

Other writing positions are more integral to company operations than technical writing. An example is contract specialist. A contract specialist assists in the preparation of new and revised insurance policy contracts, in reviewing changes in insurance laws and court decisions and recommending consequent changes in policy contracts, and in constantly analyzing information in industry news releases and publications that might affect the company. With experience and training, this person usually earns the coveted status of certified property and casualty underwriter (CPU) and advances to positions of considerable responsibility.

Some large corporations, such as General Mills, General Foods, and Borden, have organized staffs that do nothing but deal with masses of inquiries received daily from the consumer public. At Borden, a division manager heads a consumer communications system and is responsible for a "consistent, prompt, professional reply to all consumer written and telephone inquiries." Written replies must be sent within ten days. These inquiries are estimated to total 100,000 annually. The manager supervises a staff of nine employees to do the job: two professional correspondents, two associate correspondents, one telecommunications correspondent, and four writers. The job description of one of the professional correspondents, who is personally responsible for about 1,500 letters annually, indicates that he or she helps train two of the four correspondents on the staff and supervises their work in handling 62,000 "original responses" annually.

Many companies have writing positions in the area of employee relations or personnel services. Borden has a policy and program specialist, who "performs assignments in researching, developing, writing, and recommending corporate personnel programs and policies for company-wide use and distribution." This person works under the supervision of a personnel services representative, who is "responsible for writing, editing, and publication of the employee communications program."

Finally, there are writing-related (and teaching-related!) jobs in the area of education and training. Some large companies have training specialists for this purpose. These "specialists" develop training programs in such areas as orientation and safety, the use of special equipment, the learning of basic technical skills, and management techniques. Their duties are generally outlined in the job description chapter under the heading "Training Specialist." More specifically, the duties of an insurance firm's life sales educator are these, in part:

- Develops and prepares training material for sales schools, clinics, seminars, self-study, and any other applicable educational techniques for use in regional, district, and agents' offices.
- Constructs training-meeting agendas and scripts for instructors.
- Creates visual aids to be used with scripts in meetings and conferences.
- Maintains and institutes improvements, corrections, and additions in all text material and training programs for life sales.
- Assists in the development and production of audiovisual sales, training aids, and point-of-sale visual aids.
- Participates in the development of tests and surveys related to life insurance training.

Although the personnel managers of some large organizations cannot seem to think of a thing if asked about writing-related positions (even recent inquiries have drawn enigmatic blanks from such industrial giants as Coca-Cola, Dupont, Emerson Electric, Global-Marine, Kodak, and Georgia-Pacific), obviously all of them, regardless of their business, have one or more types of these jobs. Firms as diverse as the Chase Manhattan Bank, Dekalb Ag-Research, Diamond Shamrock, Allis-Chalmers, and General Mills *all* have writing jobs in publications and in public relations. At least three of the companies mentioned above (Farmer's Insurance Group, Armco Steel, and General Electric) have positions in all of the areas described. Farmer's Insurance Group itself lists ten separate job descriptions, and Armco Steel lists eighteen. General Electric, at last report, carried on its payroll over a thousand people in writing-related positions. If these companies are representative of business as a whole, and they certainly appear to be, it is a good bet that a person with good writing and editing qualifications and the willingness to do some looking will be able to turn up a suitable job in the foreseeable future.

English Majors and the Job Market

It seems only fitting to conclude with a word regarding how English majors have fared during the recent years of high nationwide unemployment. Although nothing approaching adequate data on this subject is available, a recent survey in which the English departments of sixteen colleges and universities participated is quite encouraging.[8] These institutions are located in Arkansas, the District of Columbia, Iowa, Mississippi, New York, North Carolina, Ohio, Pennsylvania, Texas, Utah, and West Virginia.

Somewhat surprisingly, considering the tightness of the teaching job market, the survey revealed that one year after graduation 38% of the former English majors of these institutions held full-time teaching positions in public or private schools at the secondary level, and some chairs noted that more graduates might have found teaching jobs had they only gone where the openings were; 31% had chosen to continue their education in professional or graduate schools (18% in English); 5% had not sought employment, primarily because of marriage; and the remaining 26% had succeeded in becoming employed in nonteaching jobs of one kind or another. Most surprisingly, none of these departments reported complaints that their students had a hard time finding jobs. On the contrary, an Ohio college observed that, as a result of some departmental career counseling, "several of our majors sought and got jobs in areas which had heretofore not entered their thinking." And speaking of counseling, the only complaint (one that English teachers in public schools as well as in colleges and universities ought to take very seriously) came from a college junior who wondered why no one had told him earlier of the value of English: "Why do not high school and college counselors make these facts known? Why did I have to wait until my third year of college to find out that English majors can do something besides teach or work on a newspaper staff? It seems to me that in this age of growing unemployment, people in the world of education should try harder to communicate to students all the possibilities of their major." Perhaps those who have read this pamphlet will help to remedy this situation.

The toughest challenge was faced by PhDs fresh out of graduate school with nowhere to go; but even they, according to a survey conducted in 1981 by the Modern Language Association, weathered the storm admirably, switching to alternative careers in as many as sixteen professional areas, including advertising, banking, business management, editing, government, law, library sciences, public relations, technical writing, and television. Nearly 70% reported that they were completely satisfied with their new careers.[9] One such PhD, Ellen Berland Sachar, found herself featured in a *TV Guide* article (22 November 1980). Sachar exchanged teaching for Wall Street, did her apprenticeship as a junior stock analyst assigned to the publishing industry, and soon rose to the position of senior

TV-broadcasting-stock analyst with a large brokerage house.

A few English departments have conducted studies to learn more specifically what kind of nonteaching employment their majors have found following graduation. That of the University of Southern Mississippi English Department revealed that many had been successful in a remarkably broad range of areas.

Perhaps the most successful of these graduates in terms of income is a young man who as an undergraduate was a straight A "double major" (English and business administration). He had a choice of several good job offers, accepted a position with a large oil company in Houston, Texas, and reportedly is doing very well. Another, after earning a master's degree in English and teaching for a short time, entered law school and is now a prominent young attorney. Several other more recent graduates are now in law school.

At least three recent graduates with English master's degrees have turned to federal service and now hold GS-9 and GS-11 positions. One of the three, a GS-11, is nevertheless completing her doctorate and, if circumstances permit, may return to teaching. If not, she need not worry; she has already established a promising career with the government. A number of other graduates with baccalaureate degrees are in various entry-level positions, having scored well on the entrance examination.

Several USM English graduates who included advanced composition, creative writing, and technical writing in their undergraduate curricula have taken jobs as technical writers with large industries (one a giant shipbuilding firm). One young woman became a television commentator and interviewer and received a civic Outstanding Woman of the Year Award. Another young woman proudly described her good fortune in a "thank you" note to the English department: "I finished my English degree in November with intentions of going into advertising or public relations. After checking the occupational horizon, I went to see South Central Bell. I am now a district public relations supervisor. I am making a good salary in a good job."

A young man who was in the ROTC as an undergraduate decided to become a career officer in the United States Army. He has written, "My English degree not only has trained me so that I can compete with my contemporaries but has even placed me ahead of them in many instances." Further, his wife, another USM English major, scored exceptionally well on the entrance examination and occupies a civil service position at the post where her husband is located.

A few doctoral candidates have understandably considered it expedient to switch to other professional areas that have promised good opportunities for employment after a relatively short period of additional graduate training. One such student decided to take a master's degree in counseling. Unfortunately, upon graduation she found that the promises of quick employment had been somewhat exaggerated. There were few good openings and many applicants for every available position. At this time, however, the state legislature established a new agency, the Department of Youth Services, and a person was sought who not only had training in counseling but was capable of handling administrative paperwork and public relations material (the position has been dubbed "counselor-writer-in-residence"). She easily beat out her competitors, but she alone had, in addition, a master's degree in English and experience in teaching composition. When last heard from she was completely happy with her work. Two PhDs, having taught a number of years in unsatisfactory locations, turned to law careers. One graduated from the LSU School of Law fifth in her class, Order of the Coif, and is now practicing law in Baton Rouge; the other is in the process of completing her law degree.

Finding suitable employment is perhaps hardest for young married graduates who are restricted to the areas in which their spouses are working, especially if teaching jobs are limited. Two USM graduates in this situation discovered for themselves the practical value of what the above surveys have shown to be the English major's most cherished attribute: the desire and the ability to continue to learn. One applied to a Delco Remy company for an advertised payroll and accounting position—a brave move in view of the fact that her college work included no accounting, computer, or advanced mathematics courses. After fourteen grueling hours of interviews and a crash course in the use of the computer and accounting procedures, she was informed that she got the job (1) because she had the requisite college degree and (2) because she could take instruction. The experience of the second graduate was even more unusual. Her husband is employed in Biloxi, Mississippi, where a large military installation, Keesler Field, is located. After exhausting all other possibilities, she applied for a position on the base, hoping feebly that there might be an opening at the post library. To her surprise she was offered the position of training instructor in electronics. It was no mistake. The official letter stated, "We know you have no background in electronics, but your record indicates that you are highly trainable." After a course of instruction she began as a GS-7 and has been promoted to a GS-9. Her own comment sums up appropriately the experience of all these graduates: "So, you see, my liberal arts English degree is quite salable on today's job market."

And much more might be said—for example about attractive starting salaries and such other large and inviting career areas as local and state government, national youth organizations, philanthropic foundations, and educational foundations—but the foregoing material, though brief, provides ample evidence that English majors have a bright future, if they choose, outside the four walls of a classroom. The education that they receive is not only culturally and intellectually priceless but, in the workaday world, solidly practical.

Representative Job Descriptions

For the information of both precollege and college students who might not have easy access to occupational reference works,[10] it has been considered wise to conclude with descriptive accounts of several positions that were among those most frequently mentioned as entry-level possibilities by personnel managers of private industry and the federal government. Although there has been some editing to eliminate "local" references and highly technical terms, these job descriptions follow closely those which a number of business organizations and governmental agencies were kind enough to provide for this purpose.

If students whose high anticipation exceeds their patience or who have heard accounts (possibly exaggerated) about beginning positions of specially trained colleagues should feel that some of these jobs are beneath the dignity of a college graduate, let them keep in mind these three points. First, regardless of their potential, they cannot expect to step into a supervisory spot until they have proved themselves at a lower level and learned operational fundamentals. Second, many of these jobs, particularly the more routine ones, are classified as good proving grounds from which one may well rise to positions of greater responsibility and increased personal challenge. And, finally, at the time when these positions were listed (along with scores of others), their starting salaries not only well surpassed those of public school teachers but in many instances were equal to or greater than those of college instructors, who must have at least a master's degree.

Part I Private Industry[11]

Advertising Assistant

General Description: The advertising assistant, under the supervision of the director of public relations, participates in various activities relating to advertising, publications, press relations, and public relations. After a period of from six to eighteen months, depending on his or her development, the assistant should qualify for promotion to a journeyman level as a press relations supervisor, advertising writer, or publicity writer. (See the similar position, press relations assistant.)

Specific Duties: Many of the duties are basic and routine. The advertising assistant writes articles, flyers, and brochures, assists in the production of such "deadline" projects as weekly sales department flyers, and maintains the departmental photo library; assists in such public relations matters as making arrangements for visitors and members of the press on special occasions, welcoming them, and taking them on tours of the installation; and carries out such projects as assembling existing data, charts, and photographs (with introductory remarks, captions, etc.) into brochures for presentation to interested groups of buyers.

Special Qualifications: Candidates should have a college liberal arts degree (preferably in English, speech, or journalism) and must have the ability to express themselves readily, clearly, and concisely both orally and in writing.

Buyer Trainee

General Description: A key figure in the retail business, the buyer, working under the supervision of or in cooperation with a sales staff, keeps an organization adequately stocked with merchandise that can be retailed readily and profitably.

Specific Duties: The buyer locates and develops product sources, makes contact and negotiates with manufacturers, presents new merchandise lines to store managers, informs salespersons of the special qualities or characteristics of products to be marketed, prepares forecasts and merchandise commitments, and analyzes and evaluates sales, customer demand, quality standards, delivery, and packaging.

Most organizations assign the beginner to an experienced buyer, for about a year and a half, to learn the principles of the job. Following this initial period, the trainee is promoted to assistant buyer and given responsibility for a specific line of merchandise. Those who have an aptitude for the work and have supervisory potential continue to assume increased responsibility until, after about five years, they become buyers.

Special Qualifications: A college degree, an even temperament, and the ability to meet and converse with people easily.

Claim Adjustor Trainee

General Description: A key figure in the world of casualty insurance, the claim adjuster determines the amount a company should pay claimants who have suffered loss or damage.

Specific Duties: Claim adjusters are given thorough training for this position, both in classes and on the job. They spend the first few weeks working with an experienced field claim representative, examining scenes of accidents, interviewing witnesses, and studying medical reports. They then attend formal classes in insurance law, contract law, methods of investigation, anatomy, and making automobile repair estimates. Then they are assigned to a claim post in a specific area and eventually may be promoted to supervisory positions.

Special Qualifications: A liberal arts education is desirable as well as an attractive personality and the ability to meet and work easily with strangers.

Copywriter

General Description: Copywriters work in advertising. They produce sales promotion literature suitable for newspaper advertisement, advertisement by direct mail, audiovisual presentation, and house magazine articles. They may be employed either by a company or by an advertising agency.

Specific Duties: Copywriters keep informed regarding

the cost of various types of advertising, the audience that they intend to reach and influence, and the most effective means of reaching the largest segment of this group. They maintain a thorough and intimate acquaintance with the use, potential, and competitive advantages of their company's products and set forth this information in nontechnical language that is at once well-organized, interesting, easily comprehensible, and persuasive. They design rough layouts of printed literature, work with commercial artists in the preparation of finished layouts, review final artwork, and work closely with the printing services in producing the finished copy. They verify the accuracy of the material that is used and secure the necessary clearances. In addition, they attend to such routine duties as procedure writing, preparing notices for the firm's personnel, and composing letters and bulletins having to do with sales and promotion.

Special Qualifications: A liberal arts college degree, a creative mind, and a flair for colorful, memorable phraseology.

Customer Service Representative

General Description: Many large manufacturers have customer service representatives, who serve as intermediaries between the producing units of the organizations and the purchasers. This position is sometimes listed as sales correspondent and expediter.

Specific Duties: Customer service representatives receive purchase orders, keep accurate records of them, and take the necessary steps to fill them (usually by writing "mill orders" to the appropriate departments); coordinate shipping dates with the department concerned to ensure that goods can be delivered on time to the customer, and by means of follow-up memorandums and telephone calls make sure that delivery is made on the dates promised; and prepare monthly reports on order volume, take inventories, and maintain price bulletin files.

Special Qualifications: Applicants should have a college degree, preferably with a liberal arts major, should be good at detail work, should work well under pressure, should be able to communicate quickly, accurately, and effectively, orally and in writing, and should have supervisory potential.

Editor, Book Publishing

General Description: The keystone of the editorial arch is the position unqualified by an adjective, or which may be called "sponsoring editor" or "subject editor." This editor is the manager of a publishing program, responsible for the planning, development, and execution of a segment of the firm's total operation. As a manager, the editor is expected to produce a contribution to the company's revenues, profits, and growth through the employment of many resources to achieve a preconceived product and market objective.

Specific Duties: An editor produces organized infor-
mation, usually (but not always) developed through the efforts of outside authors, and usually (but not always) presented in printed form. This process demands a creative faculty in designing and planning publishing programs, a critical faculty in evaluating with detachment new works or works in progress, an analytical faculty in sorting out the signals from the marketplace, and an organizational faculty in molding the final product.

Special Qualifications: A liberal arts college degree, preferably with some course work in journalism, and previous editorial experience at lower levels. Usually (but again, not always) editors come to their positions from other positions in publishing.

Editor, House Publication
(Company Newspaper)

General Description: The editor is responsible for the editing and the makeup of the company newspaper, which has as its objective the publication of news relative to the company and its employees.

Specific Duties: The editor keeps in close touch with all levels of personnel in the company in order to remain abreast of operations, products, employee activities, and other items of potential publication value; is responsible for the collection and final preparation of all material that is to be used, such as feature stories, articles, announcements, personals, editorials, and photographs; rewrites articles when necessary and makes sure that all material is written in proper form for publication and is accurate; supervises all personnel engaged in gathering news items; is responsible for getting all copy to the printer ahead of the deadline; and works with the printer in making up the publication.

Special Qualifications: Some formal schooling in journalism and three or more years of experience in newspaper reporting and makeup. There is often a training period, too, of three to six months. During this period, the editor sometimes carries the title of plant communications trainee.

Editorial Supervisor, Book Publishing

General Description: The editorial supervisor (copy editor, depth editor) is responsible for the work of converting manuscripts into published books. The degree of detail ranges, according to needs in individual cases, from substantial "in-house" rewriting ("depth" editing) to simply marking the manuscript with typesetter's instructions.

Specific Duties: Almost all manuscripts are subjected to the ministrations of a copy editor, who is responsible for improving clarity, for removing inconsistencies and redundancies, for establishing uniformity of style, and for providing proper instructions for composition as specified by the typographical designer.

Special Qualifications: At least a liberal arts degree with a concentration in English and journalism. Many publishers employ free-lancers for these functions. The particular skills of the English major are essential, whether or not they were acquired through formal academic training.

Management Trainee

General Description: The management trainee is given a training program designed to provide the knowledge and experience (often in various phases of the company's management) prerequisite to promotion to management positions.

Specific Duties: Trainees are assigned to such departments as credit, sales, engineering, advertising, accounting, traffic, warehousing, or personnel, where they perform various duties under the close supervision of seasoned administrators. In each department they observe techniques utilized by experienced workers, learn line and staff functions, perform specific departmental duties, and become familiar with the effect of management policies and viewpoints on each phase of business operations. Trainees' assignments may be rotated among all departments or among departments having allied functions. The length of time spent in each department varies but is normally six months.

Special Qualifications: In addition to a college degree, trainees must have sufficient independence to proceed alone and unguided, for much of their work eventually is in problem areas. They must be able to remain cool under fire and to make decisions quickly and with a high degree of accuracy. Inasmuch as they deal with much confidential information, they must also be discreet.

Methods Analyst (Manuals)

General Description: Working under general supervision, the Methods Analyst (Manuals) organizes, edits, and controls the correct documentation of company policies and procedures through the proper maintenance of company manuals.

Specific Duties: The analyst reviews and analyzes existing documentation of company policies and procedures, initiating corrective action where discrepancies exist; coordinates documentation of policies and procedures with representatives of the departments concerned; provides technical writing assistance in the form of editing by revising, classifying, simplifying, amending, and improving the language, readability, and consistency of the policies and procedures; and supervises the publication of the material for company use, including preparation of written material, art work, layout, format, and related details.

Special Qualifications: A college degree, preferably in English, and a solid grammatical background. Course work or experience in technical writing, rewriting, and editing is especially desirable.

Personnel Representative

General Description: The principal function of the personnel representative (known also as a personnel specialist) is to assist a company in filling vacancies.

Specific Duties: Personnel representatives consult with managers concerning needs in various areas and seek to meet those needs, usually by listing openings with employment agencies; receive and screen applicants; refer some for testing where appropriate; interview and test some types (such as clerical help) themselves; refer others, such as those with qualifications for administrative or technical positions, to interviewers who are more experienced in those areas; and sometimes recommend possible transfers or promotions within the company's ranks. Eventually, after they have become more experienced, they may counsel, advise, and instruct employees and supervisors concerning all types of personnel actions as well as company policies and procedures, represent the personnel section in the handling of such problems as job termination, and make confidential written reports to supervisory personnel regarding employee relations.

Special Qualifications: Applicants must have a bachelor's degree, preferably with some course work in psychology and sociology, must be able to communicate with ease and accuracy orally and in writing, and, usually, must have at least one year of experience in employment activities with the company, which may be achieved by on-the-job training.

Press Relations Assistant

General Description: The press relations assistant is concerned with basic but nevertheless essential public relations activities. This position is also often listed as news writer, public relations writer, and communications specialist.

Specific Duties: The press relations assistant originates copy for, obtains approvals for, and distributes routine press releases concerning personnel appointments and company activities; maintains files of press clippings as well as files of current biographical information about company executives; researches and writes articles for the company newspaper; handles the lending of company audiovisual material; and performs miscellaneous duties assigned by the manager of press relations, such as answering requests for information about the company and its products and distributing informational materials within the corporation.

Special Qualifications: A four-year liberal arts college education, with emphasis on composition, literature, and journalism.

Production Trainee

General Description: Especially large organizations with numerous installations have on-the-job management training programs to prepare candidates to be plant superintendents. The food processing company (one of the nation's largest) that provided the details for this job description designates this position "production trainee." In many respects this position resembles that of management trainee.

Specific Duties: Under the supervision of experienced personnel, production trainees are exposed to all phases of the firm's operations for a period of about two years, spending an allotted amount of time in each major production division. They must learn how to deal with operation problems and personnel at all levels in anticipation of responsibilities to be assumed on completion of the training. They are expected to be capable of improving the management competence at the operating plants through such measures as more effective cost control, quality improvement, and utilization of equipment. During training they keep a detailed record of what they are taught and what they observe, make occasional reports to those who are in charge of the training, offer recommendations regarding areas in which they need additional experience, and evaluate the effectiveness of the training received in the assigned departments. By the end of the training period they are expected to be ready for assignment as plant superintendents and to have the potential for further advancement.

Special Qualifications: A college degree, the ability to adjust to changing situations, the ability to communicate clearly and concisely orally and in writing, the ability to cope with previously unfamiliar material, and the temperament to sustain the mental pressures that accrue as a result not only of the rigorous training program but also of working with personnel who may not be entirely sympathetic to the trainee's purpose.

Sales Trainee

General Description: The sales trainee's chief objective is to learn how to market the company products most effectively.

Specific Duties: Trainees learn how to service existing retail accounts in a particular geographical area and methods of maximizing those accounts. They also learn how to make sales presentations to new and existing customers, how to promote the products in ads, displays, etc., and how to solicit new accounts. Often they are first given a short formal training program of about three weeks, followed by programmed instruction and on-the-job training supervised by experienced salespersons. Upon completion of the training program, trainees become sales representatives. Sometimes they are furnished with company cars, and their base salary is usually supplemented by an incentive system.

Special Qualifications: A college degree (many companies prefer a liberal arts major), a pleasant, outgoing personality with the ability to meet people easily, and the potential and desire to move up in the ranks of sales management.

Systems Analyst

General Description: Working under general supervision, the systems analyst methodically examines and defines detailed computer systems to develop programs for electronic data processing. This is but one of the many computer jobs that were suggested as career possibilities for English majors.

Specific Duties: The systems analyst conducts studies of all defined systems and specifications and develops block diagrams and machine project flow charts; codes, prepares test data, tests and debugs programs, revises and refines programs as required, and documents all procedures used throughout the computer program; defines data-processing problems and devises logical procedures to solve them, keeping in mind the capacity and limitations of the equipment, operating time, and form of desired results; and, where necessary, recommends equipment modifications or additions to develop an efficient and effective system.

Many large organizations have systems-analysis training programs designed to develop middle- and upper-level management personnel, such as senior analysts, project managers, systems supervisors, technical support managers, and managers of technical services.

Special Qualifications: A college degree is desirable (though not absolutely necessary), preferably with some formal training in computer programming.

Technical Writer

General Description: The technical writer interprets, edits, reorganizes, and rewrites technical or scientific subject matter so as to render it intelligible and useful to the general reader. Although these writers are employed by a wide variety of firms, work with countless types of material, and carry numerous designations (technical writer–field service, technical writer–manuals, technical writer–marketing, engineering writer), the following specific description provided by an aeronautics corporation is typical of the group.

Specific Duties: Technical writers gather necessary information from such sources as blueprints, schematics, actual equipment, and direct contact with engineering, production, customer relations, or vendor personnel. They must, of course, become familiar with pertinent specialized terminology and be able to determine when information furnished them is inadequate or misleading. They must be able to organize and present this information in a clear and concise manner, maintaining established editorial standards and conforming to company, customer, or (in some cases) military specifications. The results of their efforts include technical engineering manuals; instruction leaflets, bulletins, and handbooks; parts lists and catalogs; engineering reports; company advertisements; publicity releases; motion pictures; and transparency slides for use in sales promotion.

Special Qualifications: A college degree in English, journalism, or engineering is necessary. An English major should have some background work in technical areas simply to become familiar with basic scientific terminology; a major in a technical field should have at least an English minor, with emphasis on composition. In addition, there is usually a training period of six months to a year, during which employees learn about the company's equipment and organization and their specific duties.

Training Specialist

General Description: It is apparent from the preceding job descriptions that many large companies have extensive training programs. To develop, conduct, and coordinate these programs in accordance with a company's requirements and policies is the responsibility of the training specialist.

Specific Duties: Training specialists develop training programs in such areas as orientation and safety, the use of special equipment (including computers), management, and the learning of basic technical skills; determine the training methods to be employed; prepare lesson plans, diagrams, charts, and other visual aids; prepare training manuals; both instruct and supervise instruction; maintain records regarding course content, effectiveness of instruction, and the progress of the trainees; and compile and organize data relative to training needs.

Special Qualifications: Minimum requirements are a college liberal arts degree with training in curriculum instruction and visual aids, three to four years of full-time teaching experience. and supervisory ability. A master's degree in English and education or just in education is desirable.

Part II: Federal Service[12]

Administrative Assistant

General Description: The multiplicity and complexity of the administrative problems constantly confronting major federal agency executives require the services of trained managerial personnel to share the burden. This is the job of the administrative assistant.

Specific Duties: Although the specific duties of administrative assistants vary according to the agency for which they work, they usually deal with administrative matters in two or more of the following areas: budgetary and fiscal, personnel, management analysis, correspondence, organization, procedure, supply, and record keeping. Such positions exist in all government agencies and range in grade from GS-5 through GS-18. Consequently, opportunities for advancement beyond entry level for those who perform effectively are excellent.

Special Qualifications: To qualify, the candidate must have completed four years of college, be eligible for the GS-5 or GS-7 grades, and be able to handle paperwork readily and accurately. Although not required, formal instruction in public administration, business administration, industrial engineering, or political science is beneficial.

Bank Examiner Trainee (Federal Reserve System)

General Description: At least once annually every state-chartered bank that is a member of the Federal Reserve System must be examined to determine the soundness of its operation. This job is the responsibility of the district Federal Reserve Bank's bank examination department. Examining personnel are first trainees, then assistant examiners, and eventually examiners.

Specific Duties: The bank examiner determines whether a given bank's loans are collectible, its investment securities sound and readily marketable without loss, its management capable, its accounting system accurate and adequate, its capital satisfactory and liquidity ample, and its operation in compliance with applicable laws and regulations.

Newly appointed staff members spend their first six to eight months learning the fundamentals. They take a four-week special course of instruction at the offices of the Board of Governors of the Federal Reserve System in Washington, work with mortgage loans, and learn how to carry out the more routine aspects of bank examination. Having successfully dealt with this phase of the work, they advance to investment examination, then to earnings, and finally to report work. When they have demonstrated that they can complete the report of a smaller bank, they are promoted to assistant examiners. After accumulating further knowledge and experience, they progress to reports of larger banks and loan work, and thence to assignments as examiner-in-charge of examination of smaller banks, under the supervision of an experienced examiner. Finally, after attending an advanced school in bank examination in Washington and being judged fully qualified, they are promoted to examiners.

Special Qualifications: A college degree and the aptitude for close, painstaking, routine work.

Budget Analyst (or Budget Examiner)

General Description: Budget analysts participate in the planning and use of financial resources needed to carry out the purposes of the agency. They often begin by occupying an entry-level trainee position designed for a person with no prior experience in budget analysis. Duties are chosen so as to expose them to all phases of the budget cycle as well as to provide instruction in the basic principles of budget analysis. Formal training courses are alternated with on-the-job training. Advancement is predicated on ability to absorb the necessary training and to assume greater responsibility.

Special Duties: Assignments include a broad range of basic tasks involving the agency's operations budgets and are designed to familiarize trainees as much as possible with standard guidelines, such as budgets and reports of previous years, agency circulars, appropriation acts, appropriate subcommittee hearing transcripts, and agency policy statements. Trainees prepare worksheets using data taken from the budget of the previous year, review portions of requests for funds, and assist in the development of budget estimates. Eventually they help determine the agency's financial needs, establish spending programs, and draft new budgets.

Special Qualifications: The candidate must have a bachelor's degree and meet eligibility requirements for the GS-5 or GS-7 grades.

Building Management Officer

General Description: Building management officers are essential figures in the operation of Veterans Administration Hospitals. As members of the hospital director's staff, they plan, organize, direct, coordinate, and control all activities within the building management division.

Specific Duties: Beginning as trainees, building management officers receive instruction in both the theory and the practice of hospital operation and gain on-the-job training in all aspects of their work. Hospital matters with which they learn to deal include interior decoration, building maintenance, and the operation of the laundry and linen service. Eventually, their duties include participating in the establishment of hospital policy, contributing to the formulation of the hospital budget, and serving on various hospitalwide committees. Following the satisfactory completion of training, candidates are usually reassigned to a position of responsibility at one of the Veterans Administration's 165 hospitals.

Special Qualifications: A bachelor's degree in any field (or equivalent experience) is required as well as GS-5 or GS-7 eligibility. Because Veterans Administration hospitals are located in many parts of the country, the candidate must also be willing and able to move from one location to another. Moving expenses are paid by the Veterans Administration, and every effort is made to locate personnel in areas of their choice.

Claims Examiner

General Description: The claims examiner, as the term suggests, processes claims related to various aspects of government service and operation. Positions of this type exist primarily in the Department of Health and Human Services, the Department of the Treasury, the Department of State, the Civil Service Commission, and the Railroad Retirement Board.

Specific Duties: The claims examiner is concerned with quasi-legal work involved in developing, examining, adjusting, authorizing, or reconsidering the settlement of claims. Depending on the agency, the claims may deal with such matters as disability, death, land, government checks, passport applications, retirement and old-age insurance, and veterans' and unemployment compensation. Experienced claims examiners may be required to obtain and evaluate all facts bearing on a claim and to evolve from these facts a written decision in accord with statutory requirements; on occasion they may even be called on to interpret the applicable laws to unions, employers, attorneys, and community groups.

Special Qualifications: To qualify for trainee status, the applicant must have a bachelor's degree with any major and be eligible for GS-5 or GS-7 grades. Opportunities for advancement to GS-9 or higher are excellent.

Educational Specialist

General Description: A person with special training in the field of education may serve the federal government in a number of ways as an educational specialist. The term includes the positions of teacher, instructor, guidance counselor, education research and program specialist, and adviser in education. Nearly every agency employs persons in this capacity, but the majority are in the Departments of the Army, Navy, Air Force, Interior, and Health and Human Services.

Specific Duties: The educational specialist may be called on to serve as teacher, instructor, or guidance counselor in a government-sponsored school or other governmental program of education; administer a school program and supervise a teaching staff; develop audiovisual aids to education; give advice and guidance to educational and cultural agencies, administer financial support to education programs in colleges and universities, state and local schools, and nonprofit institutions; and sponsor a variety of research, developmental, and demonstration programs in education in cooperation with colleges, universities, and state agencies.

Special Qualifications: The candidate must have four years of college training with any major, provided that the course of study includes pertinent preparation in the field of education. Some positions also require evidence of competence in a particular subject field, such as English.

Management Analyst

General Description: Through the efforts of the management analyst, agency executives constantly scrutinize the operations of their offices and work toward developing and improving administrative organization, methods, and procedures.

Specific Duties: As entry-level trainees, management analysts receive both formal and on-the-job instruction in basic management analysis work. They learn how to evaluate management policies and practices for the purpose of recommending improvements and how to develop work simplication programs; work measuring systems; filing, correspondence, and records systems; and communications control. Some of their work involves compiling information through research and organizing it into properly documented reports to be submitted to management analyst superiors.

Special Qualifications: The candidate must have four years of college study in any major field and must meet eligibility requirements for the GS-5 and GS-7 grades.

Management Intern

General Description: Management internships have

been developed to provide on-the-job training to superior college graduates who have the potential to advance rapidly to highly responsible managerial positions.

Specific Duties: Management interns are given a demanding twelve- to eighteen-month training program that exposes them, by means of planned rotational assignments, to the various administrative facets of the agency, such as organizational management, personnel relations and supervision, data systems, financial management, and specialized program areas. Most work assignments consist of special projects that familiarize the intern with the agency's programs, policies, operations, and procedures. The implementation of the training program is usually the responsibility of an intern coordinator, who supervises the assignment of projects, evaluates progress, furnishes guidance, and assists and coordinates the efforts of project supervisors, directly under whom interns work and to whom they regularly report. When the program is completed, interns are assigned to a permanent position, if possible to an office of their choice.

Special Qualifications: Candidates must be highly recommended by persons who have a direct knowledge of their education and experience, pass an oral examination in the form of a group discussion, and, for a GS-7 rating, have a bachelor's degree (or four years of responsible experience or a combination of such education and experience). With an additional year of graduate study, they may qualify for a GS-9 rating.

Personnel Management Specialist

General Description: The responsibilities of the personnel management specialist lie chiefly in the areas of employment, compensation, employee relations, and training.

Specific Duties: The trainee, usually under the direct supervision of higher-grade specialists, is given both formal instruction and on-the-job experience in such duties as determining job requirements, classifying positions, planning recruitment, determining training needs, establishing coordination with employee organizations, counseling employees, analyzing turnover problems, working out disciplinary matters, gathering and analyzing salary and wage data, and preparing well-organized and meaningful reports either for oral briefings or for submission in writing to higher administrative echelons.

Special Qualifications: The candidate must have four years of college training with any major and have GS-5 or GS-7 eligibility.

Public Information Specialist

General Description: The public information specialist collects and disseminates information regarding all aspects of an organization's activities.

Specific Duties: Public information specialist trainees, having first become thoroughly familiar with the organization and services of the agency to which they have been assigned, perform such basic tasks as maintaining comprehensive mailing lists to assure adequate press coverage; screening the *Congressional Record* for items of interest to the agency; scanning various daily and weekly publications for items of interest to the agency; handling routine inquiries and correspondence regarding the programs of the agency; and, eventually, assisting in the preparation of appropriate material for newspapers, radio, television, periodicals, and federally published pamphlets.

Special Qualifications: The applicant should have a bachelor's degree, preferably with a concentration in English and journalism, and GS-5 or GS-7 eligibility.

Writer and Editor

General Description: Writers and editors—serving under the more specific position designations of writer, editor, radio scriptwriter, motion picture scriptwriter, television scriptwriter, and technical editor—perform the important task of maintaining good communication between American citizens and their government. There are over four thousand such positions distributed throughout governmental agencies.

Specific Duties: These duties vary widely, of course, according to the special function of the employee and the nature of the organization. The following are those duties outlined for a technical editor assigned to the Small Business Administration: edits draft manuscripts as assigned by the principal technical editor; under the principal editor's supervision and general instruction, makes necessary deletions and changes to adapt copy to the format of the specific series assigned; performs editorial research to revise and update the Small Business Bibliographies, such as footnotes and portions of text; reviews and verifies bibliographical references for accuracy of title, author, date of issue, price, publisher's name and complete address; researches for current availability of such listings to determine if they are pertinent to the particular subject being presented; researches for and extracts specific case examples for use in editing management publications; evaluates applicability of such reference material to specific projects; exercises individual initiative and ingenuity in proposing a suitable format to give an effective presentation; with knowledge of the specific publication requirements, marks up copy for the proper style and format within the limitations of each series; attaches camera copy for artwork and other necessary changes on copy, prepares requisition and other supporting forms, and completely arranges the manuscript copy for the typesetter; prepares charts, tables, and forms for special presentations in accordance with space and style limitations, verifies reference material used, checks headings and footnotes, and ensures proper placement in the text for overall continuity.

Special Qualifications: Naturally, applicants must have a well-developed ability to write clear and interesting prose. In addition, they must have bachelor's degrees and GS-5 or GS-7 eligibility.

Notes

[1] The term *business* is defined very broadly, to include every type of commercial activity as well as finance.

[2] Obviously it is not possible to recognize here all of the college administrators, business executives, and federal agencies who contributed to this study, but a special note of gratitude is in order to the following for their unusual interest and cooperation: Camille W. Cook, assistant to the dean, University of Alabama School of Law; Orley R. Lilly, Jr., chair, Admissions Committee, University of Tulsa College of Law; A. E. Papale, dean, Loyola University School of Law; James C. Quarles, dean, Walter R. George School of Law, Mercer University; Ernest A. Raba, dean, School of Law, St. Mary's University; Roy L. Steinheimer, Jr., dean, Washington and Lee University School of Law; D. J. Klepper, dean, University of New Mexico School of Medicine; Horace N. Marvin, dean, University of Arkansas School of Medicine; Frank N. Miller, associate dean, George Washington University School of Medicine; Robert L. Tuttle, academic dean, Bowman Gray School of Medicine; William Austin, president, Gaffers and Sattler, Incorporated (a subsidiary of Magic Chef, Inc.); Richard L. Hankinson, director, personnel division, Blue Cross and Blue Shield Hospital Service Incorporated of Iowa; Edward Mandt, personnel manager, Borden, Incorporated; Harris Shane, vice-president, industrial relations, Pullman, Incorporated; John Kadow, assistant postmaster general, Management Information Systems Department, United States Postal Service; John W. Murtha, director, Office of Recruitment and College Relations, United States Civil Service Commission; and Gordon S. Pressley, chief, Staffing Division, United States Civil Service Commission, Atlanta Region.

[3] "Restless Employees," *Wall Street Journal* 18 Sept. 1967: 1; J. Sterling Livingston, "The Troubled Transition," *Journal of College Placement* April-May 1970: 35-41.

[4] Charles B. Stoll, "Book Publishing Career for English Majors," *ADE Bulletin* 33 (1972): 49-51.

[5] Respondents were asked to assign a 1, 2, or 3 to each item to indicate its first, second, or third importance. The results were totaled and averaged, the lowest averages indicating the highest rankings.

[6] Notice the emphasis on special training in the job descriptions listed beginning on p. 21.

[7] The Department of Justice and the Department of Agriculture declined to participate in the survey.

[8] As were the surveys mentioned earlier, this one was privately conducted by the author. The number of questionnaires apologetically returned incomplete indicated, unfortunately, that the majority of English departments do not know what their former graduates are doing and are taking no steps to find out.

[9] "Survey of PhD's in Alternative Careers," *MLA Newsletter* 13.2 (Summer 1981): 10-11.

[10] Such as *Occupational Outlook Handbook*, published annually by the United States Department of Labor, Bureau of Labor Statistics, or *The Encyclopedia of Careers and Vocational Guidance*, ed. William E. Hopke, 2 vols. (Garden City: Doubleday, 1967).

[11] The following business organizations contributed information on which these job descriptions are based: Ampex Corporation; Electrical Components, Launch Support, and Avionics Divisions of the Bendix Corporation; The Boeing Company; Crown Zellerbach Corporation; Honeywell, Incorporated, EDP Division; Johnson and Johnson; Kaiser Aluminum and Chemical Corporation; LTV Aerospace Corporation; Monsanto Company; The Nestlé Company; Oscar Mayer and Company; Sperry Rand Corporation, Univac Division; State Farm Insurance; Stokely-Van Camp, Incorporated; and Welch Foods, Incorporated. The job descriptions of editor, book publishing, and editorial supervisor, book publishing, are taken from Stoll, with his permission.

[12] Sample federal service job descriptions are based upon actual job descriptions furnished by various agencies and upon information in the following booklets: *Federal Service Entrance Examination, Announcement No. 410* (Washington: US Civil Service Commission, 1972); *From College to Career with the Federal Government* (Atlanta: Atlanta Region, US Civil Service Commission); *After College What? OPI-40* (Washington: Small Business Administration, 1969); *Building Management Officers*, VA Pamphlet 10-65 (Washington: Veterans Administration, 1969); and *Help Us to Meet the Challenge* (Washington: US Dept. of Labor, 1970).

ALABAMA
Southerland Bldg.
806 Governors Dr., SW
Huntsville 35801
(205) 453-5070

ALASKA
Federal Bldg.
701 C St., Box 22
Anchorage 99513
(907) 271-5821

ARIZONA
US Postal Service Bldg.
522 N. Central Ave.
Phoenix 85004
(602) 261-4736

ARKANSAS
Federal Bldg., Third Floor
700 W. Capitol Ave.
Little Rock 72201
(501) 378-5842

CALIFORNIA
Linder Bldg.
845 S. Figueroa
Los Angeles 90017
(213) 688-3360

1029 J. St., Rm. 202
Sacramento 95814
(916) 440-3441

880 Front St.
San Diego 92188
(714) 293-6165

211 Main St., Second Floor
San Francisco 94105
(415) 974-9725

COLORADO
1845 Sherman St.
Denver 80203
(303) 837-3509

CONNECTICUT
Federal Bldg., Rm. 613
450 Main St.
Hartford 06103
(203) 722-3096

DISTRICT OF COLUMBIA
1900 E Street, NW
Washington 20415
(202) 737-9616

FLORIDA
Federal Bldg. and U.S.
   Courthouse
80 N. Hughey Ave.
Orlando 32801
(305) 420-6148 or 6149

GEORGIA
Richard B. Russell Federal
   Bldg., Ninth Floor
75 Spring St. SW
Atlanta 30303
(404) 221-4315

GUAM
Pacific News Bldg.
238 O'Hara St., Rm. 308
Agana 96910
344-5242

HAWAII
Federal Bldg., Rm. 1310
300 Ala Moana Blvd.
Honolulu 96850
(808) 546-8600

ILLINOIS
55 E. Jackson, Rm. 1401
Chicago 60604
(312) 353-5136

INDIANA
46 East Ohio Street,
Rm. 124
Indianapolis 46204
(317) 269-7161

IOWA
210 Walnut St., Rm. 191
Des Moines 50309
(515) 284-4545
In Scott and Pottawattamie
counties call (402) 221-3815.

KANSAS
One-Twenty Bldg., Rm. 101
120 W. Market St.
Wichita 67202
(316) 269-6106
In Johnson, Leavenworth, and
Wyandotte counties dial (816)
374-5702.

LOUISIANA
F. Edward Hebert Bldg.
610 South St., Rm. 849
New Orleans 70130
(504) 589-2764

MARYLAND
Garmatz Federal Building
101 W. Lombard St.
Baltimore 21201
(301) 962-3822

MASSACHUSETTS
McCormack Bldg.
Post Office and Courthouse
Boston 02109
(617) 223-2571

MICHIGAN
477 Michigan Ave., Rm. 565
Detroit 48226
(313) 226-6950

MINNESOTA
Federal Bldg.
Ft. Snelling
Twin Cities 55111
(612) 725-4430

MISSISSIPPI
100 W. Capitol St., Suite 335
Jackson 39260
(601) 960-4585

MISSOURI
Federal Bldg., Rm. 134
601 E. 12th St.
Kansas City 64106
(816) 374-5702

Old Post Office, Rm. 400
815 Olive St.
St. Louis 63101
(314) 425-4285

NEBRASKA
US Courthouse and Post
Office Bldg., Rm. 1010
215 N. 17th St.
Omaha 68102
(402) 221-3815

NEW HAMPSHIRE
Thomas J. McIntyre Federal
   Bldg., Rm. 104
80 Daniel St.
Portsmouth 03801
(603) 436-7220 ext. 762

NEW JERSEY
Peter W. Rodino, Jr.,
   Federal Bldg.
970 Broad St.
Newark 07102
(201) 645-3673
In Camden dial (215) 597-7440

NEW MEXICO
Federal Bldg.
421 Gold Ave. SW
Albuquerque 87102
(505) 766-5583

NEW YORK
Jacob K. Javits Federal Bldg.
26 Federal Plaza
New York 10278
(212) 264-0422

James N. Hanley Federal Bldg.
100 S. Clinton St.
Syracuse 13260
(315) 423-5660

NORTH CAROLINA
Federal Bldg.
310 New Bern Ave.
PO Box 25069
Raleigh 27611
(919) 755-4361

OHIO
Federal Building
200 W. 2nd St.
Dayton 45402
(513) 225-2720

OKLAHOMA
200 NW 5th St., Rm. 205
Oklahoma City 73102
(405) 231-4948

OREGON
Federal Bldg.
1220 SW 3rd St.
Portland 97204
(503) 221-3141

PENNSYLVANIA
Federal Bldg., Rm. 168
Harrisburg 17108
(717) 782-4494

Wm. J. Green, Jr., Fed. Bldg.
600 Arch St.
Philadelphia 19106
(215) 597-7440

Fed. Bldg.
1000 Liberty Ave.
Pittsburgh 15222
(412) 644-2755

PUERTO RICO
Federico Degetau Federal Bldg.
Carlos E. Chardon St.
Hato Rey 00918
(809) 753-4209

RHODE ISLAND
John O. Pastori Federal Bldg.
   Rm. 310, Kennedy Plaza
Providence 02903
(401) 528-5251

SOUTH CAROLINA
Federal Bldg.
334 Meeting St.
Charleston 29403
(803) 724-4328

TENNESSEE
100 N. Main St., Suite 1312
Memphis 38103
(901) 521-3956

TEXAS
1100 Commerce St., Rm. 6B4
Dallas 75242
(214) 767-8035

701 San Jacinto St.,
Fourth Floor
Houston 77002
(713) 226-2375

643 E. Durango Blvd.
San Antonio 78206
(512) 229-6611

VIRGINIA
Federal Bldg., Rm. 220
200 Granby Mall
Norfolk 23510
(804) 441-3355

WASHINGTON
Federal Bldg.
915 2nd Ave.
Seattle 98174
(206) 442-4365

WEST VIRGINIA
Federal Bldg.
500 Quarrier St.
Charleston 25301
(304) 343-6181 ext. 226

Appendix B
College Honor Societies Acceptable under the Superior Academic Achievement Standard

Alpha Chi
Alpha Epsilon
Alpha Epsilon Delta
Alpha Kappa Delta
Alpha Kappa Mu
Alpha Omega Alpha
Alpha Pi Mu
Alpha Sigma Mu
Alpha Sigma Nu
Beta Gamma Sigma
Beta Kappa Chi
Beta Phi Mu
Chi Epsilon
Delta Epsilon Sigma
Delta Mu Delta
Delta Phi Delta
Delta Sigma Rho-
  Tau Kappa Alpha
Eta Kappa Nu
Gamma Phi Epsilon
Gamma Sigma Delta
Gamma Theta Epsilon
Iota Sigma Pi
Kappa Delta Pi
Kappa Gamma Pi
Kappa Mu Epsilon
Kappa Omicron Phi
Kappa Tau Alpha
Lambda Iota Tau
Mortar Board
National Collegiate Players
Omega Chi Epsilon

Omicron Delta Epsilon
Omicron Delta Kappa
Omicron Kappa Upsilon
Omicron Nu
Order of the Coif
Phi Alpha Theta
Phi Beta Kappa
Phi Kappa Phi
Phi Sigma
Phi Sigma Iota
Phi Sigma Tau
Pi Delta Phi
Pi Gamma Mu
Pi Kappa Lambda
Pi Lambda Theta
Pi Mu Epsilon
Pi Omega Pi
Pi Sigma Alpha
Pi Tau Sigma
Psi Chi
Rho Chi
Sigma Delta Pi
Sigma Gamma Epsilon
Sigma Gamma Tau
Sigma Pi Sigma
Sigma Tau
Sigma Tau Delta
Sigma Theta Tau
Sigma Xi
Tau Beta Pi
Tau Sigma Delta
Xi Sigma Pi